for Caleb
by the grace of God, may you live up to your namesake: "my servant Caleb, who has a different spirit and has followed me fully." -Numbers 14:24

copyright 2016 by Brendan Beale. All rights reserved.

All Scripture quotations, unless otherwise indicated, are taken from the Holy Bible, New International Version®, NIV®. Copyright ©1973, 1978, 1984, 2011 by Biblica, Inc.™ Used by permission of Zondervan. All rights reserved worldwide. www.zondervan.com The "NIV" and "New International Version" are trademarks registered in the United States Patent and Trademark Office by Biblica, Inc.™

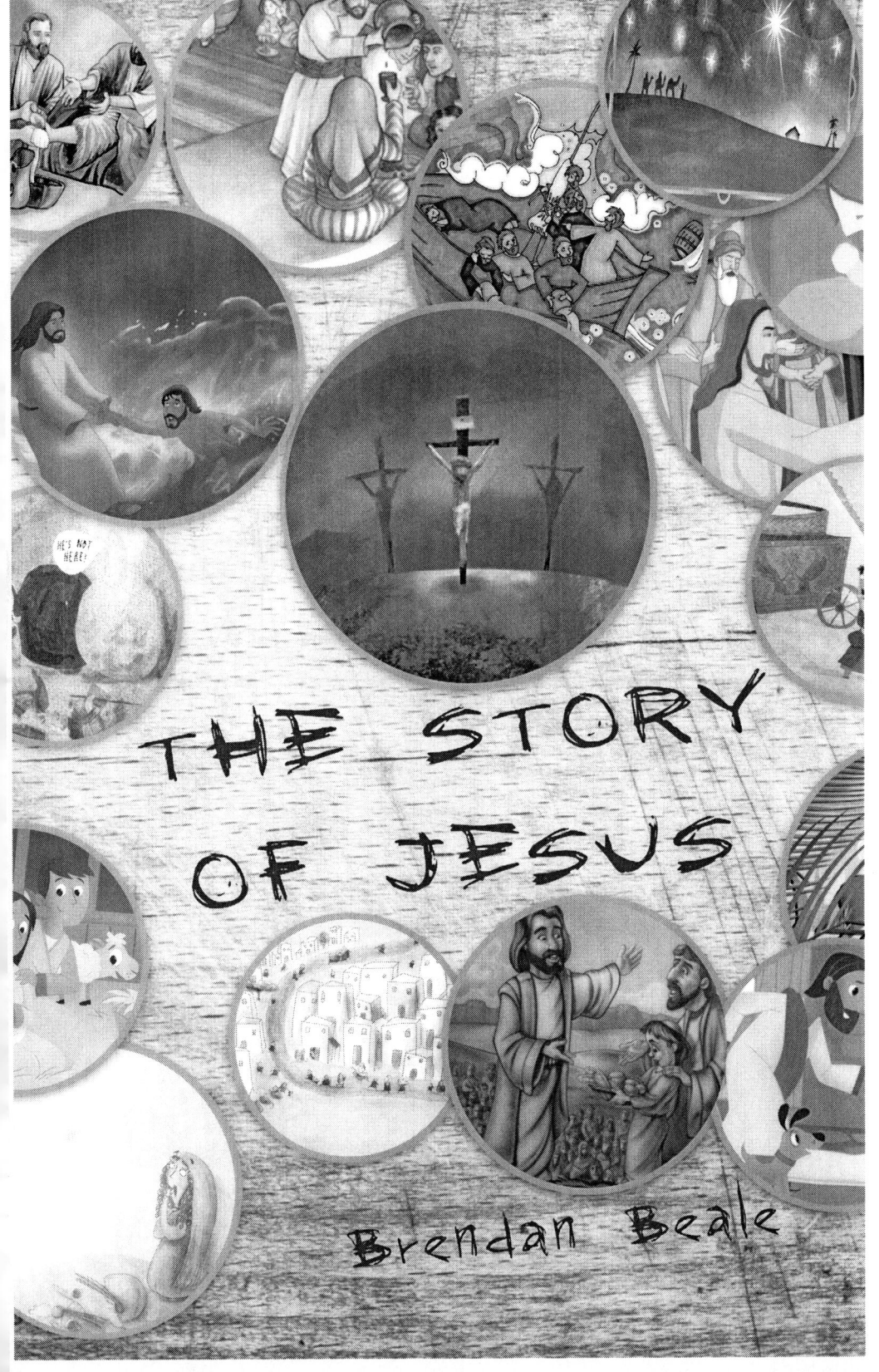

CONTENTS

Introduction for the grown-ups	1
Introduction for the kids	6
A Lame Party Turned Awesome	9
Following Jesus for the Wrong Reason	13
Not a Ghost Story	17
Jesus Loves Gross People	20
Something Scarier than the Storm	25
Honey, It's Time to Wake Up	28
The Camel Goes through the Eye of the Needle	31
Interrupting Jesus	36
The Hardest Healing	40
Finding Lost Stuff and Throwing Lots of Parties	44
No Excuses	51
Thanksgiving is About Jesus	55
Stinky Shepherds	58
The Backwards, Upside-Down King	62
The Missing Nativity Piece	66
King of Kings	71

You can't sit on the Fence	75
God Growing Up	79
Taking the Test for You, Part 1	83
Taking the Test for You, Part 2	86
Here comes the Kingdom	89
A Lousy Bunch of Losers	92
The Real Celebrity	97
The Bad Guys	100
The Future came Early	103
Here comes the King	109
A King Who Serves	112
Scared Jesus	116
The King on the Cross	121
The Most Natural Thing in the World	125
The Best Prank Ever	128
The Half-Empty Glass	133
Jesus on the Loose	137
The King Sits Down	140
WIJD?	143
The King Coming Back	147

introduction for the grown-ups

Hi there, parents and teachers! (Kids, you can skip the boring grown-up talk and go to your own introduction).

Let's get straight down to business: we've been getting the story of Jesus all wrong, and I think it's killing our own walk with Christ and our efforts to disciple our kids.

Sound harsh? Let me back up and explain. If your experience of growing up in the church was anything like mine, you probably remember Sunday School lessons with flannelgraph and cheesy songs and little moral lessons. Don't get me wrong: flannelgraph is a brilliant invention, and I love cheesy songs (I'm the cheesiest person I know, just ask my wife). And lessons in morality are important. But the way I learned the Bible was mostly as a story of lessons with a moral point: David trusted God, so I should trust God. Adam and Eve disobeyed God, and that's bad, so I should obey God. Jesus loved people, so I should love people.

Now those are all true points, and valid applications of Scripture. Jesus did love people, and 1 John 4:19 says that's why I should love people too. But in presenting the stories of Scripture as primarily moral lessons, what happened inadvertently was that the gospel ended up getting reversed. And the grand, unifying point of the Bible was no longer "This is what God has done for you in Christ." Instead, it somehow became, "This is how you should live."

It's not that it's wrong to teach our children to obey God or to love others. Those are in fact important lessons. But our children are wired from birth as legalists and world-lovers, ingrained down to their DNA. And so all our efforts as parents and teachers and Sunday school teachers—whatever form children's discipleship takes in your season of life—must be bent towards shaking them loose from their legalism with the radical grace of the gospel and wooing them from their world-loving with the superior joy of knowing Jesus.

I don't think anybody set out to mess up my theology. Most of my Sunday School teachers were, I'm sure, godly people who loved Jesus. But somehow, without anyone ever intending it, this moralism had just become the default atmosphere of children's ministry. And as I've talked to people, and visited churches, I've realized that this wasn't my unique experience. This is how most people were taught the Bible: as a set of rules, and a collection of stories telling us to be better. Somehow, somewhere along the line, we got everything backwards.

Is it any wonder, then, that studies show that up to 70% of our young people, when they graduate high school, leave the church and don't return—if they return at all—until they are married with children? The reason our kids are leaving is not because they didn't learn how to be good; it's because their hearts were never captured by the greatness and glory of Jesus Christ. We've made the goal of parenting and children's ministry the goodness of our kids rather than the glory of Jesus wrecking and remaking their lives.

That's the point of the quadruple portrait of Jesus in the gospels: not simply that we would learn to live better, but that the glory of Jesus would shine off the pages and pierce our hearts with his matchless beauty. All true Christian transformation starts there. "Beholding the glory of the Lord, we are being transformed into his likeness," 2 Corinthians 3:18 says. Beholding is becoming; the more we look, the more we become like.

That's the intention of this book. The book starts with an assortment of Jesus' miracles and parables so that we would wowed by the utter uniqueness of the God-man. And then, beginning with the Christmas story and moving chronologically through the life of Christ, we see the unveiling of the gospel as the humble King moves relentlessly towards the cross and empty tomb.

A couple notes on how to read this book: I've tried to write in a way that would be accessible and helpful for elementary and middle schoolers, but the book is probably helpful in different ways to different age groups. For middle schoolers, this might be an effective tool for independent devotional time. For elementary kids, I envision adults reading this to them. I've kept each chapter brief so that this could work as a family or classroom devotional. I've also included the entire biblical text of each story, because I don't want to give the incorrect impression that my retelling of the story of Jesus is more engaging than the Bible itself. The Word of God is the real story, and it's only the Word of God that really has the power to change hearts and lives. My storytelling and exposition is merely an attempt to shine a light back onto the biblical text so that we could see more clearly the glory that is there. So don't skip the biblical text at the beginning of the chapter: that's where all the glory is.

A final note on a theme you'll start to pick up on: I've deliberately highlighted one of the primary themes of the gospels, in particular the gospel of Matthew: that Jesus is the long-awaited King. The point of all his miracles is not merely a demonstration of his power, but rather an unveiling of the kind of kingdom he is bringing, and the type of king he is. You'll see that again and again in these stories, and the point I'm trying to make to kids is really the same point that the gospels are trying to make: isn't Jesus a great king, and don't you want to be a part of his kingdom?

Because after all, isn't that the truth that first drew

us into the kingdom, and what we're praying will capture the hearts of our kids? Jesus is a great king. And his already-present and still-coming kingdom is a great kingdom. Come on in.

introduction for the kids: being wowed by Jesus

"Do you have eyes but fail to see, and ears but fail to hear? And don't you remember?" –Mark 8:18

Everyone loves a good story, right? Even if you don't like to read (which you should! reading is awesome!), movies tell stories too. So think about your favorite story. Good stories grab your attention, pull you in, and make you start getting excited about the characters and what happens to them. And the best stories—the ones that really stick with you—even change the way you look at everything around you.

But for some reason, when we come to the greatest story about the greatest character in the whole world, we get bored. The greatest story in the whole world is the story of Jesus—who he is, what he's done, how wonderful he is. And yet sometimes we're like, "Yawn, Jesus… I know those stories."

I think the reason that we sometimes get bored with the stories of Jesus is because we've been reading them wrong this whole time. It might not be your fault; to be honest, grown-ups get this wrong a lot, too. You may have heard a story of Jesus' life in Sunday School, for example, and the teacher told you, "Now children, you see how Jesus was nice to that person. You should be nice to that person." And it almost feels like the story is wagging a finger at you, saying, "Yeah, shape up and start acting more like Jesus."

If that's how you've heard the story of Jesus before, I'm sorry. Because that's backwards. Of course we should be nicer. But the point of the story of Jesus isn't so that we'd learn how to be better, or nicer, or kinder. The point is for us to be wowed by Jesus.

Because Jesus is flat-out, blow-your-mind awesome. He does things that no one else could possibly do. He says things that no one else says. He treats people the way no one else treats them. He is so powerful and yet so humble. He's so strong and yet so gentle. He's honestly kinda scary (at least to the bad guys), and yet he's the kindest, most loving person who has ever lived. Seriously, no one is like him, even a little bit. He's in a category of awesomeness all by himself.

So here's the point of reading all the stories: Jesus is the most amazing main character of any story ever told… and these stories are all real, and Jesus is still alive today. When we're reading the stories of Jesus' life, we're reading about someone—the best Someone in the whole world—whom we can really know. We can't walk up to Jesus and shake his hand like people could when he was on earth, but here's the thing: we still can "see" Jesus. We can see him in the stories recorded in the Bible. It's in these stories that Jesus—who is alive today—still speaks to us and shows us what he's like.

But there's a difference between seeing these stories and *really* seeing them. Jesus said that every person has two sets of eyes: one set of eyes in your head, and another set of "eyes" in your heart. The eyes in your head are for looking at stuff; the eyes in your heart are for really understanding and loving what you've seen. It would be possible to read all the miracles of Jesus and still come away saying, "Cool story, bro, but who cares?" In fact, that's what a lot of people who saw the miracles firsthand said. They saw Jesus raise the dead and heal lepers and feed whole crowds, but they weren't impressed—or even worse, they were impressed for the wrong reasons. The miracles didn't make them love Jesus, or trust Jesus, or worship Jesus. And that's because they were only looking with the first set of eyes—the ones in their head—and not looking with the eyes of the heart. Jesus said to them, "You have eyes, but fail to see. You have ears, but you fail to hear." They saw all the miracles, but missed the main point.

So please, don't miss the main point. Ask God to open the eyes of your heart to see how amazing Jesus really is, so that you can be wowed by Jesus.

And then settle in, and get ready to meet the greatest person in the history of the world.

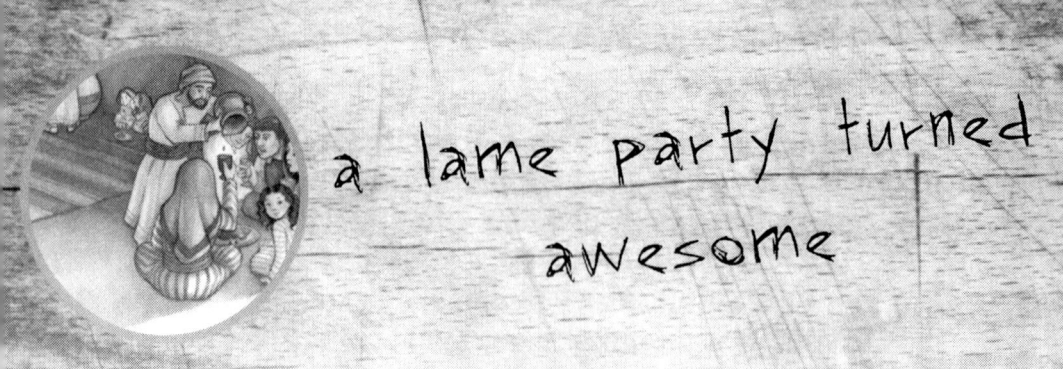

a lame party turned awesome

On the third day a wedding took place at Cana in Galilee. Jesus' mother was there, and Jesus and his disciples had also been invited to the wedding.
When the wine was gone, Jesus' mother said to him, "They have no more wine."
"Woman, why do you involve me?" Jesus replied. "My hour has not yet come."
His mother said to the servants, "Do whatever he tells you."
Nearby stood six stone water jars, the kind used by the Jews for ceremonial washing, each holding from twenty to thirty gallons.
Jesus said to the servants, "Fill the jars with water"; so they filled them to the brim.
Then he told them, "Now draw some out and take it to the master of the banquet."
They did so, and the master of the banquet tasted the water that had been turned into wine. He did not realize where it had come from, though the servants who had drawn the water knew. Then he called the bridegroom aside and said, "Everyone brings out the choice wine first and then the cheaper wine after the guests have had too much to drink; but you have saved the best till now."
What Jesus did here in Cana of Galilee was the

first of the signs through which he revealed his glory; and his disciples believed in him. –John 2:1-11

Have you ever heard the expression, "First impressions are everything?" It means that when you meet someone for the first time, what you say and do tells them a lot about who you really are. That's why your mom is always saying how it's important to try to give a good first impression.

Jesus' very first miracle is our "first impression" of him. He could have chosen to do any sort of miracle, but he picked this one to show us what he's like, almost like he's saying, "Hi, my name is Jesus, and this is what I'm like."

So if you were Jesus, what miracle would you choose as your "first impression?" How would you reveal to everyone what you're like? Would you raise somebody from the dead, or calm a storm, or do something even more spectacular, that would make everyone say, "Wow!"? Or maybe you could heal a sick person, or help someone who is hurting, so everyone would know how much you cared.

Jesus did all those miracles and many more, but they weren't what he chose to do first. In fact, the very first miracle he chose to do was something very surprising: he took a lame party and made it awesome.

Yep, that's what his first miracle was: taking a lame

party and making it awesome. He was at a wedding (which, as you know, are parties all about love and joy and dancing!), and the wine ran out. Back in Jesus' day, the wine was a really important part of the party; it was the only thing they had to drink, and the whole party would be ruined if they ran out.

So what did Jesus do? He had the servants fill up some water jars, and suddenly, almost before anyone noticed, the water had turned to wine. And not just any wine; it had turned into the best, most expensive and delicious wine anyone had ever tasted.

The people at the party were blown away by how good this wine was. They had never tasted anything so good. "Where did this wine come from?" everyone kept asking. But the only people who had seen what really happened were the servants who had filled up the jars of water, and Jesus' disciples who were with him.

That's how Jesus chose to reveal himself to his disciples. Of all the things he could have done, that's what he chose as his first impression: taking a lame party and making it awesome. So why water into wine? Why this miracle?

Each one of Jesus' miracles tells us something about him. That's why Jesus did all of his miracles: so that we would understand what he's like, how great and wonderful he is. That's the point of this first miracle too; Jesus made this lame party awesome because he wants us to know something really important about what kind of King he is, and what kind of Kingdom he was bringing. He wants us to know that he is a King of joy and gladness, and his kingdom is a celebration. Jesus was coming into a world full of sadness and hurt and death and sin, and he was bringing hope and joy and life and healing and forgiveness. The kingdom of God is a party, a victory celebration over sin and death and darkness, and Jesus is the life of that party.

That's the kind of King Jesus is, and the kind of kingdom he was bringing. That's what his first miracle tells us, and that's what every other miracle was about, too. Everywhere Jesus went, that kingdom started coming, and the party started expanding. Sick people got better. Sinful people found mercy. Broken, hopeless people found joy and purpose. Funerals were turned into celebrations when dead people came back to life. And the party just kept getting bigger and bigger.

Welcome to God's kingdom.
Isn't Jesus a great king?

following Jesus for the wrong reason

The people asked Jesus, "What sign then will you give that we may see it and believe you? What will you do? Our ancestors ate the manna in the wilderness; as it is written: 'He gave them bread from heaven to eat.'"
Jesus said to them, "Very truly I tell you, it is not Moses who has given you the bread from heaven, but it is my Father who gives you the true bread from heaven. For the bread of God is the bread that comes down from heaven and gives life to the world."
"Sir," they said, "always give us this bread."
Then Jesus declared, "I am the bread of life. Whoever comes to me will never go hungry, and whoever believes in me will never be thirsty."
–John 6:30-35

The story of Jesus feeding five thousand with a couple of loaves and fishes is actually a kind of sad story. I mean, it's a cool story too, and I definitely would have liked to have been there to see it. I would have loved to see what it looked like for food to multiply in the baskets as it was passed out. But it's a sad story because of what happened afterwards: people missed the point of Jesus completely.

You see, after Jesus fed all those people, the crowd was understandably wowed. They even wanted to make him king. But they were impressed for the wrong reason: they just wanted a king who would give them stuff. So Jesus abruptly left.

The next day, the crowd tracked him down and demanded another miracle. You might have thought Jesus would be impressed with how diligently they searched him out, but he wasn't. "You were looking for me," Jesus said, "not because of the miracle I did, but just because you wanted more food. Stop working for food that spoils, but instead work for the food that lasts forever."

Jesus knew that the crowd was only looking for him because they wanted another show, another miracle, another meal. He knew they didn't actually care about him; they only wanted what he could give them.

The conversation went on, with the people demanding another miracle (as if yesterday's miracle wasn't impressive enough), and Jesus telling them that the real bread that God wanted to give them was the kind of food that would last forever.

That got the crowd's attention. "Okay," they said. "Give us that bread!"

Jesus answered, "I'm the bread of life. Whoever comes to me will never go hungry, and whoever believes in me will never thirst." In other words, what Jesus was saying was, "I'm the only thing that will satisfy you forever."

The crowds only wanted Jesus because Jesus could give them stuff. But Jesus was here to give them something far, far better: the gift of himself. Jesus knew that all the other stuff we could possibly want—food, toys, clothes, money, friends, family—will never make us happy in a way that would last. Toys break, food spoils, clothes go out of style, money just makes you miserable, people disappoint you. But we were created to know and love Jesus, and to be known and loved by Jesus, and only that can fill us up with happiness forever.

But the crowds following Jesus didn't want to know and love Jesus. They just wanted him to give them stuff. And that's why this turns out to be a sad story. They missed the whole point of Jesus: that the best possible gift he came to give was the gift of himself. That only he could fill them up with happiness forever. That he was the Person that they were created to know and love and enjoy forever.

So here's a question to think about: why do you want to follow Jesus? So that he can bless you and give you stuff? Do you think that if you're good, God will give you all the things you pray for? If so, you're acting like the crowds in the story. They didn't actually want Jesus; they only wanted what Jesus could give them. Or do you want to know and love Jesus more? Is that what you pray about? I hope so, because that's the kind of prayer that Jesus loves to answer.

not a ghost story

Immediately Jesus made the disciples get into the boat and go on ahead of him to the other side, while he dismissed the crowd. After he had dismissed them, he went up on a mountainside by himself to pray. Later that night, he was there alone, and the boat was already a considerable distance from land, buffeted by the waves because the wind was against it.
Shortly before dawn Jesus went out to them, walking on the lake. When the disciples saw him walking on the lake, they were terrified. "It's a ghost," they said, and cried out in fear.
But Jesus immediately said to them: "Take courage! It is I. Don't be afraid."
"Lord, if it's you," Peter replied, "tell me to come to you on the water."
"Come," he said.
Then Peter got down out of the boat, walked on the water and came toward Jesus. But when he saw the wind, he was afraid and, beginning to sink, cried out, "Lord, save me!"
Immediately Jesus reached out his hand and caught him. "You of little faith," he said, "why did you doubt?"
And when they climbed into the boat, the wind

died down. Then those who were in the boat worshiped him, saying, "Truly you are the Son of God." –Matthew 14:22-33

Most of the time when this story is told, the focus is on Peter and how, when he saw the wind and the waves, he stopped looking at Jesus and started to sink. So, then, the point is: keep your eyes on Jesus even when it's scary, and everything will be okay.

But while I guess that's true, that's not the point of the story. The point of the story isn't to teach us something to do, it's to teach us something about Jesus. So instead of shaking our finger at Peter for his weak faith, let's stand back and be amazed by Jesus.

And we should be amazed, because, c'mon: Jesus is *walking on water*. How cool is that? I tried that at the pool once. It didn't work; I went straight to the bottom. And yet Jesus, seemingly without any effort, is just trotting out across the lake, not minding the wind and the waves at all. Who needs a boat when you're Jesus? Seriously, this is a pretty impressive miracle.

But I think even more wonderful than the miracle is Jesus' heart behind the miracle. His friends had been trying to row across the lake all night, and were being battered by wind and waves and were getting nowhere. They had left the shore that previous afternoon, expecting to get to the other side by night time. What was supposed to be a relatively quick trip across the lake had turned into a nine-hour nightmare. They must have been exhausted, hungry, and maybe even a little frightened.

Jesus sees them struggling, and so what does he do? He goes to help them. That's what this story is really about. It's about Jesus caring about his friends who are in trouble. And it's about Jesus coming to do what they couldn't do for themselves. They thought they were on their own, out of Jesus' reach. They were wrong. They thought they could get to the other side with their own strength. They were wrong about that too. Peter thought he could walk on the water without keeping his eyes fixed on Jesus. And, yep, he was wrong about that, too.

The disciples had forgotten that Jesus was the One who had fed 5,000 people with a couple loaves of bread (in fact, that was what had happened just before this story, that same day). They thought Jesus could take care of all those other people, but that he couldn't take care of them. But Jesus wanted to show them that they were never beyond his reach, that they needed him just as much as all those hungry people, and that he was perfectly capable of taking care of them too. And Jesus wanted them—and us— to know that even if the situation looks bad, we're never, ever alone.

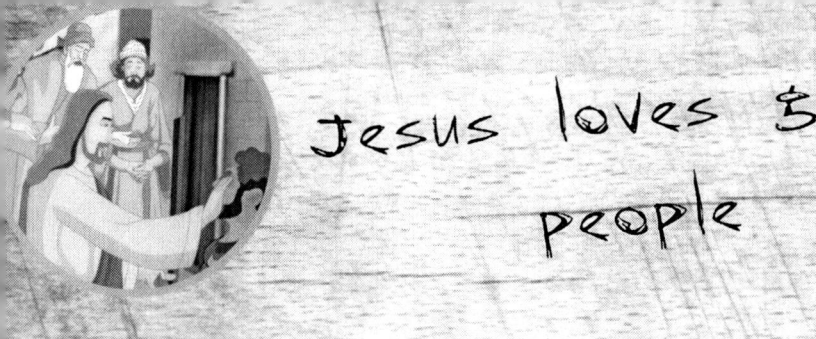

Jesus loves gross people

A man with leprosy came to him and begged him on his knees, "If you are willing, you can make me clean."
Jesus was moved with compassion. He reached out his hand and touched the man. "I am willing," he said. "Be clean!" Immediately the leprosy left him and he was cleansed.
Jesus sent him away at once with a strong warning: "See that you don't tell this to anyone. But go, show yourself to the priest and offer the sacrifices that Moses commanded for your cleansing, as a testimony to them."–Mark 1:40-45

In order to understand how wonderful this story is, you first have to understand leprosy. Leprosy is a terrible disease that slowly eats away at your flesh, making it start to rot and fall off. It was a slow disease; it would start as a rash, but over the course of weeks, months, and years, it would spread and get worse and worse, even to the point of fingers and ears and noses falling off. Gross, right? Leprosy victims were in terrible pain and horribly disfigured—that means, their faces got all messed up—and eventually, they would die from the disease. It was one of the most feared diseases of biblical times. (By the way, today there is medicine that quickly treats leprosy, and it's not around so much anymore, so you don't need to worry about catching it!)

But the worst part of leprosy, even worse than the fingers falling off and your face rotting away, was that leprosy victims couldn't be around anyone else. This was to keep other people from getting sick. And in the days before hospitals and doctors, if you got leprosy, you had to leave your family and your friends and go live by yourself, or with other lepers. You couldn't be around healthy people. A leper wouldn't even be allowed to come in to the synagogue or temple to worship God! In fact, if a leper saw a healthy person coming towards them, the law said they had to call out, "Unclean, unclean!" to warn them away.

So imagine for a moment that you had leprosy, and think about how terrible it would be. You would have lots of pain. You would look worse and worse (and feel worse and worse) as the disease spread all around your body. And you couldn't be with your friends or family at all. In fact, most of them would probably be scared to come near you. You would be all alone. No one could even touch you. Think about that! No hugs when you were feeling sad, no goodnight kisses, no handshakes, no wrestling around with friends, no pats on the back. How would that make you feel?

So in this story, when we meet a man with leprosy, that's what's going on. His face and skin is decaying and rotting away. It's probably been years since he has seen his family, or slept in his own bed, or been able to have a job, or felt the touch of another person.

Remember, he's not supposed to come near or talk to anybody. But when he hears that Jesus is coming, he's so desperate that he decides to break all the rules. He runs (or, probably, limps) up to Jesus and falls down to his knees in front of him. He knows Jesus can do amazing things. Maybe, just maybe, he thinks, Jesus would be willing to help him. "If you are willing," he says to Jesus, "you can make me clean!"

There was a pause as Jesus looked at him. The crowd around Jesus, who probably scattered as soon as they saw the leper coming, held their breath and waited to see what Jesus would say. Would he yell at the man? Would he tell him to get lost and not come near again? Would he lecture him about breaking the leprosy rules?

Jesus looked at the broken, disfigured man in front of him, and didn't do any of those things. Mark chapter 1 says that Jesus was "moved with compassion." His eyes welled up with tears. His heart ached for all the pain and sorrow this man had experienced. He looked at the poor, helpless man in front of him, and he loved him. Jesus loved this disgusting, diseased leper.

And then he did something that no one had ever done before, something that probably made the crowd gasp in horror. Jesus reached out his hand… and *touched* the man. How many years had it been since the man had felt the touch of another person? No one was brave enough to even look at his twisted, rotting face, let alone touch him. But here was Jesus, completely unafraid, loving this man in a way that no one dared to.

The leper probably looked up at Jesus in shock. He probably wanted to shout, "Don't touch me, Jesus! I'll infect you!" But to his surprise, Jesus was smiling. "I am willing," Jesus said gently. "Be clean!"

All at once, a warm feeling spread through the man's arms and legs and all around his body. Fingers and toes that he hadn't been able to feel anymore tingled back to life. The roaring pain in his face and arms died away. The leper looked down at his hands. A moment ago, they had been red and black and cracked and oozing. Now the skin was soft and smooth like a baby's. He felt his face. The wounds and scars were healed. The leprosy was completely gone!

The compassion of Jesus in this story is amazing. Jesus loved people that no one else would even look at. He loved the unlovable. He touched the untouchable. He forgave the unforgivable.

And today, at this moment, Jesus is still the same. He still loves people that no one else wants to. He still loves you, even though your sin is a far worse disease than leprosy. And if we come to him, asking for forgiveness for all the things we've done wrong, we'll find that he still has the same love and same answer that he gave to the leper: "I am willing. Be clean!"

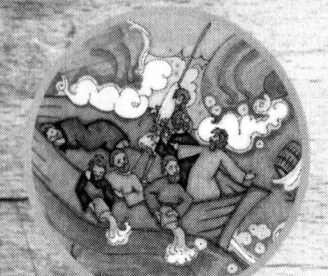

something scarier than the storm

That day when evening came, he said to his disciples, "Let us go over to the other side." Leaving the crowd behind, they took him along, just as he was, in the boat. There were also other boats with him. A furious squall came up, and the waves broke over the boat, so that it was nearly swamped. Jesus was in the stern, sleeping on a cushion. The disciples woke him and said to him, "Teacher, don't you care if we drown?"
He got up, rebuked the wind and said to the waves, "Quiet! Be still!" Then the wind died down and it was completely calm.
He said to his disciples, "Why are you so afraid? Do you still have no faith?"
They were terrified and asked each other, "Who is this? Even the wind and the waves obey him!"
–Mark 4:35-41

Next time that there's a thunderstorm, try to do this: go outside in the middle of the rain and lightning, look up at the clouds, and say, "Storm! Stop it!" See if it works.

It probably won't. Because the storm doesn't care

what you say. It's a lot bigger and stronger than you, so you can stand there and yell and holler and stamp your foot, and it will just keep thundering.

That's why this story in Mark 4 is so impressive. Jesus had been snoozing in the boat during their little pleasure cruise, until an enormous storm blew up out of nowhere. The disciples, most of whom had been fishermen their whole lives, were used to storms, but they had never seen a storm like this. Within a few minutes, the waves were pouring into their little fishing boat, and they were starting to sink. The disciples began panicking. If something didn't happen soon, they were going to die.

So they woke Jesus up. He stood up, stretched, yawned, glanced up at the raging storm, and said, "Quiet!" And just like that, the clouds scurried away apologetically, the wind vanished, and the waves disappeared.

Now, if you were one of the disciples, what do you think your reaction would have been? Would you have jumped up and down for joy? Given Jesus a big hug and thanked him for saving your life? High-fived all your buddies in the boat? Asked Jesus how he did that neat trick?

Surprisingly, the disciples didn't do any of those things. In fact, they didn't seem very happy at all. During the storm, they had understandably been afraid. But now that the sun was shining, Mark 4 says, "they were terrified." Somehow, they were more afraid now than when the boat was filling with water.

Why? Mark 4:41 gives us the answer: "They were terrified, and asked each other, 'Who is this? Even the wind and the waves obey him!'" Something scarier than the storm was in the boat with them. They knew their Old Testaments; they knew that Psalm 89 says, "Who is like you, LORD God Almighty? You, LORD, are mighty, and your faithfulness surrounds you. You rule over the surging sea; when its waves mount up, you still them." They realized that this was no mere man in the boat; this was the Lord God Almighty himself. And that's pretty scary to be standing in a boat with the God of the universe.

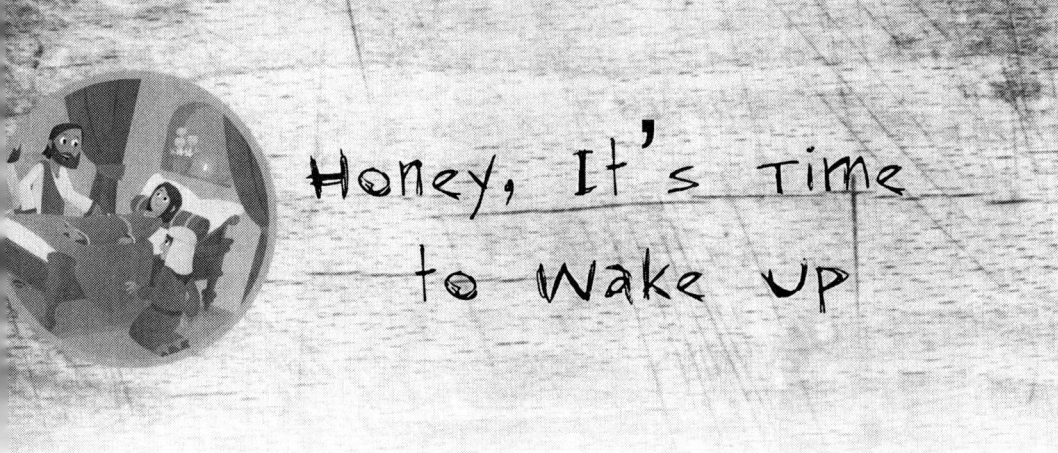

Honey, It's Time to Wake Up

While Jesus was still speaking, some people came from the house of Jairus, the synagogue leader. "Your daughter is dead," they said. "Why bother the teacher anymore?"
Overhearing what they said, Jesus told him, "Don't be afraid; just believe."
He did not let anyone follow him except Peter, James and John the brother of James. When they came to the home of the synagogue leader, Jesus saw a commotion, with people crying and wailing loudly. He went in and said to them, "Why all this commotion and wailing? The child is not dead but asleep." But they laughed at him.
After he put them all out, he took the child's father and mother and the disciples who were with him, and went in where the child was. He took her by the hand and said to her, "Talitha cum!" (which means "Little girl, I say to you, get up!").
Immediately the girl stood up and began to walk around (she was twelve years old). At this they were completely astonished. He gave strict orders not to let anyone know about this, and told them to give her something to eat. –Mark 5:35-43

One of the things that I love most about Jesus' miracles is how much doesn't show off when he does them. Jesus doesn't wave his hands around and shout "Abracadabra," or make long speeches or pompous prayers. He's not trying to impress the crowds. Over and over again, he does these miracles simply because he loves people. And when you love people, you don't have to show off or make a big deal about it. You just have to help them.

This is one of those stories. A little girl was dying, and her daddy was desperate to help her. Doctors couldn't do anything and it was almost too late, when he heard that Jesus was in town. Maybe, just maybe, if Jesus could get there in time, he would be able to help. So the daddy ran to Jesus and fell down at his feet, begging him to come and help his little girl. He didn't need to beg, though, because of course Jesus would help.

But by the time Jesus got there, it was too late. The little girl had died. Everyone was crying, and the daddy was heartbroken. He told Jesus that he appreciated him coming, but that he could leave now. After all, Jesus could do amazing things, but death wasn't something you could just "fix." But Jesus didn't seem concerned. "Don't worry," he told the grieving parents. "I'll go wake her up."

Jesus took them into the girl's bedroom. The little girl lay there, very still and cold. Jesus took her hand and, said, in a gentle voice, "Talitha cum," which, in Aramaic (the language they spoke at the time), means, "Honey, wake up." It's the same thing that a mommy or daddy would say to their little child after a nap.

That's all Jesus said. No incantations or prayers or magic words. Just, "Honey, it's time to get up." And with incredible power and tenderness, Jesus reached down into death and gently, effortlessly brought the little girl back to life. She yawned, sat up, and rubbed her eyes, as if she had just woken up from a good night's sleep. "Give this girl some lunch," Jesus said with a smile to her amazed parents.

Who else but Jesus could do something like this?

Only Jesus is powerful enough to raise the dead, and only Jesus is tender enough to do it with a gentle pat on the hand. That's what makes Jesus so amazing: he is Lord over life and death, and yet we see him down on his knees next to a child's bed, holding a little girl's hand. Jesus raises the dead the same way a mommy wakes their child from a nap. That's how gentle he is. And that's how strong he is. No one else is like him.

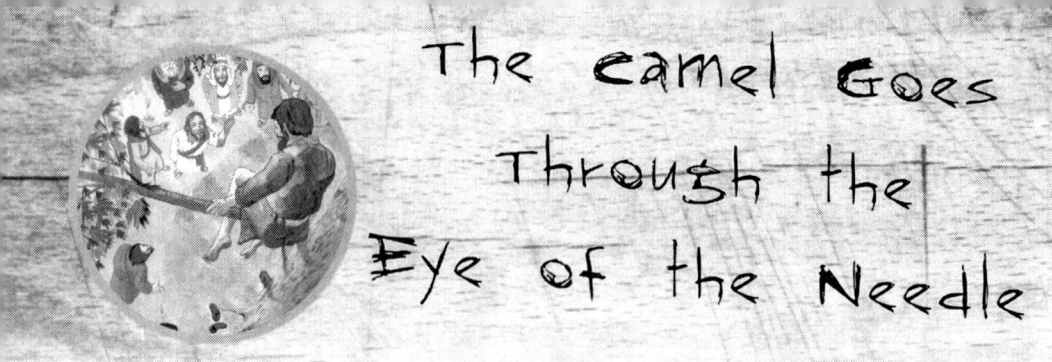

The camel Goes Through the Eye of the Needle

And a ruler asked him, "Good Teacher, what must I do to inherit eternal life?" And Jesus said to him, "Why do you call me good? No one is good except God alone. You know the commandments: 'Do not commit adultery, Do not murder, Do not steal, Do not bear false witness, Honor your father and mother.'" And he said, "All these I have kept from my youth." When Jesus heard this, he said to him, "One thing you still lack. Sell all that you have and distribute to the poor, and you will have treasure in heaven; and come, follow me." But when he heard these things, he became very sad, for he was extremely rich. Jesus, seeing that he had become sad, said, "How difficult it is for those who have wealth to enter the kingdom of God! For it is easier for a camel to go through the eye of a needle than for a rich person to enter the kingdom of God." Those who heard it said, "Then who can be saved?" But he said, "What is impossible with man is possible with God."–Luke 18:22-27

He entered Jericho and was passing through. And behold, there was a man named Zacchaeus. He was a chief tax collector and was rich. And he was seeking to see who Jesus was, but on account of the crowd he could not, because he was small in stature. So he ran on ahead and climbed up into a sycamore tree to see him, for he was about to pass that way. And when Jesus came to the place, he looked up and said to him, "Zacchaeus, hurry and come down, for I must stay at your house today." So he hurried and came down and received him joyfully. And when they saw it, they all grumbled, "He has gone in to be the guest of a man who is a sinner." And Zacchaeus stood and said to the Lord, "Behold, Lord, the half of my goods I give to the poor. And if I have defrauded anyone of anything, I restore it fourfold." And Jesus said to him, "Today salvation has come to this house, since he also is a son of Abraham. For the Son of Man came to seek and to save the lost." –Luke 19:1-10

One day, a rich young ruler came up to Jesus with a really good question. In fact, this is probably the most important question you could ever ask. And he had come to the right person. He asked Jesus, "What must I do to go to heaven?" This man was pretty proud of all the good things he did, but wanted to make sure there weren't any extra-super-holy things he was missing.

The problem was, he didn't like Jesus' answer. Jesus was able to look into this man's heart. And Jesus saw that even though this guy did lots of good, religious things, deep down he didn't really love God; what the man really loved was his money. So Jesus put his finger right on idol in this man's heart. "Give away everything you have and come follow me. Then you'll have real treasure, real wealth, in heaven."

Well, that was not the answer that the rich man wanted to hear. He had to make a choice: what would he love more—God or money? And he just couldn't bring himself to love God more. He decided he would rather have a couple years of rich living than to have Jesus and heaven forever and ever. And so he made a terrible decision: he walked away. When push came to shove, he chose his money over Jesus.

Jesus sadly watched him go. He knew that most people, if they had to choose between loving money and loving God, would rather have their money. So Jesus said, "It's hard for rich people to get to heaven," Jesus said. "In fact, it would be easier to squeeze a camel through the eye of a needle."

Jesus' friends were shocked. "Then who in the world can be saved?" they asked.

Jesus gave an amazing answer: "Nobody," he said. "It's impossible for people to save themselves. But even what's impossible is possible for God."

Now, most people think the story ends there, on a sad note. But it actually doesn't. The story keeps going, because the next day, Jesus met another rich man. And this time, the conversation went very differently.

The next day, as Jesus was coming into the city, he

met a wee little man named Zacchaeus. Zacchaeus was a rich man just like the rich young ruler before, but unlike the first man (who thought he was already a pretty good guy), Zacchaeus knew he was bad. He was a tax collector, a traitor, and a total creep. He had spent his whole career stealing money and ripping people off. Everyone who knew him hated him.

So when Jesus walked right up to him, Zacchaeus probably cringed. He probably thought Jesus was going to yell at him, or kick him out of the tree, or maybe just kick him, like everyone else did. So when, instead, Jesus said, "Zacchaeus, I'd like to have dinner at your house today," Zacchaeus's mouth probably dropped open. Why in the world would someone like Jesus want to hang out with someone like him? It was too good to be true.

But as the day went on, and Zacchaeus watched Jesus, he realized that it wasn't too good to be true. He saw Jesus heal people, and touch the untouchable, and love the unlovable... people just like Zacchaeus. Like the sun coming up in the morning, a thought started dawning in Zacchaeus's heart: "Jesus loves... me! Even me!"

And that simple, powerful truth changed everything. His whole life, Zacchaeus had loved money more than anything. He hadn't cared how many people he hurt, he just wanted to be rich. But all of a sudden he saw how much better Jesus was. And just like that, something in his heart changed. He didn't want his money anymore; he just wanted to be with Jesus. Wherever Jesus went, that's where Zacchaeus wanted to go. Whatever Jesus did, that's what Zacchaeus wanted to do to.

At dinner with Jesus that evening, he stood up and announced, "I'm done with chasing after money. I'm going to give away half of everything I own to the poor, and on top of that, I want to pay back everything I've ever stolen from anybody, and give them back four times more than I took."

Jesus smiled. "Today, salvation has come to this house, because I came here to seek and save the lost." God had done the impossible; the camel had gone through the eye of the needle; a rich person had found heaven.

Interrupting Jesus

Then they came to Jericho. As Jesus and his disciples, together with a large crowd, were leaving the city, a blind man, Bartimaeus, was sitting by the roadside begging. When he heard that it was Jesus of Nazareth, he began to shout, "Jesus, Son of David, have mercy on me!"
Many rebuked him and told him to be quiet, but he shouted all the more, "Son of David, have mercy on me!"
Jesus stopped and said, "Call him."
So they called to the blind man, "Cheer up! On your feet! He's calling you." Throwing his cloak aside, he jumped to his feet and came to Jesus.
"What do you want me to do for you?" Jesus asked him.
The blind man said, "Rabbi, I want to see."
"Go," said Jesus, "your faith has healed you." Immediately he received his sight and followed Jesus along the road. –Mark 10:46-52

I don't like to be interrupted. I think that my plans, my schedule, my ideas are important, and I don't like when people get in the way. That's probably because, deep down, I think I'm better and more special than everyone else. And if I'm better and more special, then people should get on board with what *I* want do, instead of making me stop and do what *they* want to do. (At least, that's the way I think sometimes).

But look at Jesus. Unlike me, Jesus actually IS better and more special than anyone else. His plans and his schedule and his ideas really ARE important. But when he gets interrupted—and in the gospels, it seems like he gets interrupted a lot—he never reacts the way that I usually do. Jesus is never grumpy at the inconvenience. He's never impatient with having his time taken. Even when he's in the middle of something really important, it seems like he always has time for people. He's always okay with being interrupted. And the reason why is because he loves people—really loves them. He puts their needs ahead of his own. He cares about them more than he cares about himself. People are more important to Jesus than his own plans.

That's what this story is about. Jesus was on a really important mission; he was on his final journey to Jerusalem and to the cross. This was the whole reason he had come to earth—there was nothing more important than that mission. But along the way, he came across a blind beggar named Bartimaeus. Bartimaeus (let's call him Barty) couldn't work because he couldn't see, and that meant he didn't have any money. So he didn't have anywhere to live, and most days didn't have enough food. He probably didn't have any friends either. Life was pretty hard for poor Barty.

So when Barty heard that Jesus was coming down the road, he started calling out at the top of lungs, "Jesus, Son of David, have mercy on me!" What that meant was, "King Jesus, please help me!" Barty couldn't help himself. His only hope was for Jesus to help him.

Barty was kind of loud and obnoxious, trying to get Jesus' attention, and everyone around him was annoyed. "Hush!" they said. "He doesn't want to talk to a nobody like you."

But Barty wasn't a nobody to Jesus. When Jesus heard Barty calling for him, he stopped. "What do you want me to do for you?" Jesus asked kindly.

Barty's heart leapt. "Oh please," Barty begged. "I want to see!"

Jesus smiled. "Your faith has made you better." And all at once, like the someone turning on the lights in a dark room, Barty's eyes started working again, and he could see. He laughed and cried and thanked Jesus, and immediately joined his disciples. The rest of his life, he knew, he would follow Jesus no matter what. Because Jesus, and only Jesus, had loved him enough to stop and help him.

The way Jesus treated Bartimaeus was so different than the way everyone else treated him. Jesus was patient, Jesus was kind. Jesus was willing to help. He was willing to be interrupted.

Aren't you glad that Jesus is like that? And you know what? Jesus is still like that, even today. When you pray—even little, silly prayers—he doesn't roll his eyes or check his watch. He loves you, he is patient with you, he is kind to you. So that means we can be just like Barty; any time we're in need, we can pray, "King Jesus, please help me!" And we can know that, just like with Barty, Jesus loves to be interrupted by us.

The Hardest Healing

One day Jesus was teaching, and Pharisees and teachers of the law were sitting there. They had come from every village of Galilee and from Judea and Jerusalem. And the power of the Lord was with Jesus to heal the sick. Some men came carrying a paralyzed man on a mat and tried to take him into the house to lay him before Jesus. When they could not find a way to do this because of the crowd, they went up on the roof and lowered him on his mat through the tiles into the middle of the crowd, right in front of Jesus.
When Jesus saw their faith, he said, "Friend, your sins are forgiven."
The Pharisees and the teachers of the law began thinking to themselves, "Who is this fellow who speaks blasphemy? Who can forgive sins but God alone?"
Jesus knew what they were thinking and asked, "Why are you thinking these things in your hearts? Which is easier: to say, 'Your sins are forgiven,' or to say, 'Get up and walk'? But I want you to know that the Son of Man has authority on earth to forgive sins." So he said to the paralyzed man, "I tell you, get up, take your mat and go home." Immediately he stood up in front of them,

took what he had been lying on and went home praising God. Everyone was amazed and gave praise to God. They were filled with awe and said, "We have seen remarkable things today." –Luke 5:17-26

In this story of Jesus meeting a paralyzed man, two amazing miracles took place. Do you see what they are? When the paralyzed man was first brought to Jesus, Jesus said, "Friend, your sins are forgiven." That was the first miracle. The second miracle was when Jesus healed the man so that he could walk again.

The question is, which one of those miracles do you think is more impressive? Healing a paralyzed man—that's pretty neat. With just a word, Jesus knit the man's broken spinal cord back together. Muscles that hadn't been used in years suddenly became strong. Nobody else but Jesus could do a miracle like that.

But as amazing as that was, it wasn't the most impressive miracle. The most impressive miracle was what happened when Jesus said, "Friend, your sins are forgiven." At that moment, every single bad thing that man had ever said or thought or done was immediately wiped away. His heart was cleansed of sin. He was given eternal life. His name was written down in heaven. He became God's child forever. All because Jesus said, "Your sins are forgiven."

Does that seem like a miracle to you? It is. In fact,

it's a much harder miracle than making the man walk.

Don't take my word for it; that's what Jesus himself said. The Pharisees (who thought they were super holy and better than everyone else) grumbled when Jesus forgave the man. "Doesn't he know that only God can do that?" they asked.

Jesus did know that. He knew that only God could take sin away from the heart. Only God could pay the great debt that the man owe. Only God could give him eternal life and a home in heaven.

So Jesus asked them a question, "What's easier, for me to forgive him, or tell him to walk?"

The answer is: it was much easier for Jesus to tell him to walk. All that took was just a word from Jesus. But forgiving sin is something really hard to do. In fact, it was so hard, that it would cost Jesus his life. The only way for Jesus to forgive that sin was to go to the cross and *die* for that sin, to take the punishment that the man deserved for his sin and bear it himself. Forgiving sin is the hardest thing in the whole world for Jesus to do.

But that's exactly what Jesus had come to do. He hadn't just come to heal people's sickness and make them feel better. He had come to heal a far wore disease than paralysis: he had come to heal the disease of sin. The whole point of Jesus coming to earth was to heal the disease of sin, so that everyone who trusts in him would have all their sin forgiven and a home with him in heaven forever.

So if you have trusted Jesus and asked him to forgive you, an amazing miracle has happened in your heart, too. It's the same miracle that happened in this story: God has wiped away every bad thing you've ever done or said or thought and had made you his child forever.

If you haven't asked Jesus to take away your sin, you can ask him today. You don't have to wait until you're better, or older, or smarter. Jesus has done all the hard work—he obeyed perfectly, he died for you, he rose again to life—so that all you have to do is trust him, and ask for that miracle. And then you, too, can be God's child forever.

Finding Lost stuff and Throwing Lots of Parties

Now the tax collectors and sinners were all gathering around to hear Jesus. But the Pharisees and the teachers of the law muttered, "This man welcomes sinners and eats with them."
Then Jesus told them this parable: "Suppose one of you has a hundred sheep and loses one of them. Doesn't he leave the ninety-nine in the open country and go after the lost sheep until he finds it? And when he finds it, he joyfully puts it on his shoulders and goes home. Then he calls his friends and neighbors together and says, 'Rejoice with me; I have found my lost sheep.' I tell you that in the same way there will be more rejoicing in heaven over one sinner who repents than over ninety-nine righteous persons who do not need to repent.
"Or suppose a woman has ten silver coins and loses one. Doesn't she light a lamp, sweep the house and search carefully until she finds it? And when she finds it, she calls her friends and neighbors together and says, 'Rejoice with me; I have found my lost coin.' In the same way, I tell you, there is rejoicing in the presence of the angels of God over one sinner who repents."
Jesus continued: "There was a man who had two

sons. The younger one said to his father, 'Father, give me my share of the estate.' So he divided his property between them.

"Not long after that, the younger son got together all he had, set off for a distant country and there squandered his wealth in wild living. After he had spent everything, there was a severe famine in that whole country, and he began to be in need. So he went and hired himself out to a citizen of that country, who sent him to his fields to feed pigs. He longed to fill his stomach with the pods that the pigs were eating, but no one gave him anything.

"When he came to his senses, he said, 'How many of my father's hired servants have food to spare, and here I am starving to death! I will set out and go back to my father and say to him: Father, I have sinned against heaven and against you. I am no longer worthy to be called your son; make me like one of your hired servants.' So he got up and went to his father.

"But while he was still a long way off, his father saw him and was filled with compassion for him; he ran to his son, threw his arms around him and kissed him.

"The son said to him, 'Father, I have sinned against heaven and against you. I am no longer worthy to be called your son.'

"But the father said to his servants, 'Quick! Bring the best robe and put it on him. Put a ring on his finger and sandals on his feet. Bring the fattened calf and kill it. Let's have a feast and celebrate. For this son of mine was dead and is alive again; he was lost and is found.' So they began to celebrate.

"Meanwhile, the older son was in the field. When

he came near the house, he heard music and dancing. So he called one of the servants and asked him what was going on. 'Your brother has come,' he replied, 'and your father has killed the fattened calf because he has him back safe and sound.'

"The older brother became angry and refused to go in. So his father went out and pleaded with him. But he answered his father, 'Look! All these years I've been slaving for you and never disobeyed your orders. Yet you never gave me even a young goat so I could celebrate with my friends. But when this son of yours who has squandered your property with prostitutes comes home, you kill the fattened calf for him!'

"'My son,' the father said, 'you are always with me, and everything I have is yours. But we had to celebrate and be glad, because this brother of yours was dead and is alive again; he was lost and is found.'" –Luke 15

One day, the extra-good religious people, who thought they were better than everyone else, came to Jesus. They were upset with Jesus, because he was hanging out with, well, the *wrong* kind of people. Didn't Jesus realize that he was spending time with *bad* people? He was having dinner with thieves and crooks and all sorts of other unsavory characters. And the extra-good religious people had gotten themselves all bent out of shape about this. Jesus needed to stop hanging out with sinners, they said.

What they didn't understand about Jesus was that

this was exactly why he had come: he had come to love and save sinners. He had come to offer mercy to people who knew they needed a Savior. He hadn't come to make the goody-goodies feel better about themselves; he had come to rescue the people who knew they were lost.

So Jesus told these extra-good religious people three little stories. Each story had the same point: that God loves the people you don't expect him to, way more than he should.

The first story Jesus told was about a shepherd who had a hundred sheep, but lost one. The shepherd, Jesus said, left the ninety-nine sheep to go find the lost little lamb. And when the shepherd found the lamb, he was so happy that he called together all his friends and threw a big party.

Okay, time out. Let's think about this story for a second, because it's kind of weird. I know that good shepherds always go to look for sheep who are missing, but the party at the end seems sort of strange. Why in the world would the shepherd throw a party just because one silly sheep had been found? No normal shepherd would do something like that. That one little lamb wasn't worth throwing a whole party.

But that was exactly Jesus' point. God celebrates the people you don't expect him to. Jesus said, "In the same way, there will be more rejoicing in heaven over one sinner who repents than over ninety-nine righteous persons who do not need to repent." All of heaven erupts in a party when even one sinner comes back to God and says they're sorry. Those super-good religious people looked down their noses at those "bad people," but God was throwing a party every time one of those bad people came home. You might not think that one measly sinner is worth a party, but God disagrees.

The second story goes the same way, but it's even more ridiculous: a woman who had ten silver coins lost one, and turned the whole house upside down until she found the coin. And then—get this— the woman is so excited that she calls up all her friends and throws a big party. All because she found one little coin?

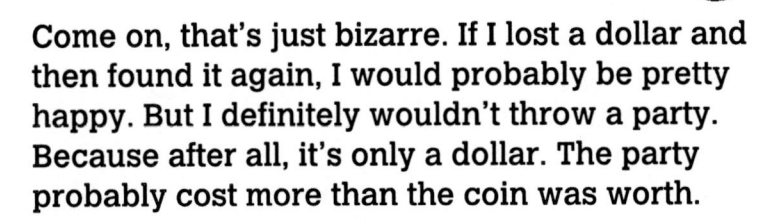

Come on, that's just bizarre. If I lost a dollar and then found it again, I would probably be pretty happy. But I definitely wouldn't throw a party. Because after all, it's only a dollar. The party probably cost more than the coin was worth.

But once again, that was exactly Jesus' point. The people we don't think are valuable are the ones God prizes the most. God is like that woman throwing a party because she found her lost coin, and the shepherd throwing a party because he found his lost sheep. He loves sinners so much more than even makes sense, and throws a party every time one of them repents.

The third story, again, tells the same lesson. Jesus tells about a son who came to his dad and basically said, "Dad, I wish you were dead so I could have all your money now." And then he takes his dad's money, runs away from home, and blows all the money on dumb stuff (what a jerk, right?). When he finally gets up the nerve to come home, he expects his dad to slam the door in his face, or maybe—just maybe—his dad would let him come home and be a servant.

But instead, the most surprising thing happens: when the son was still a long way off, his dad sees him coming and runs to him and sweeps him up in a big hug. And his dad throws a huge party to welcome his son home—the same son who had wanted him dead, stolen his money, and lost it all. Would you throw a party for someone who had treated you like that? This dad did.

The point of Jesus three stories is this: That's

exactly what God is like. He loves the people that you think are too bad to love. He loves you, even when you do bad things and break his heart. He loves you so much more than even makes sense. And when you come back to him and say you're sorry and ask for forgiveness, all of heaven erupts in a party. That's how much God loves forgiving sinners. That's how much God loves you.

No Excuses

Jesus replied: "A certain man was preparing a great banquet and invited many guests. At the time of the banquet he sent his servant to tell those who had been invited, 'Come, for everything is now ready.'

"But they all alike began to make excuses. The first said, 'I have just bought a field, and I must go and see it. Please excuse me.'

"Another said, 'I have just bought five yoke of oxen, and I'm on my way to try them out. Please excuse me.'

"Still another said, 'I just got married, so I can't come.'

"The servant came back and reported this to his master. Then the owner of the house became angry and ordered his servant, 'Go out quickly into the streets and alleys of the town and bring in the poor, the crippled, the blind and the lame.'

"'Sir,' the servant said, 'what you ordered has been done, but there is still room.'

"Then the master told his servant, 'Go out to the roads and country lanes and compel them to come in, so that my house will be full. I tell you, not one of those who were invited will get a taste of my banquet.'" –Luke 14:12-24

Jesus kept having run-ins with the extra-good religious people. These people, who thought they weren't that bad because they tried hard to keep all of God's rules, didn't realize that the sin deep down in their hearts had blinded them to the truth: that they were proud and arrogant and selfish and didn't trust God. Jesus kept trying to show them this, but they didn't want to hear it. Which I guess sort of makes sense: is that the kind of news you'd really want to hear?

This story is another story Jesus told to try to wake up these extra-good religious people. In this story, he compares heaven and the kingdom of God to a big party that a king is throwing. Jesus is the King throwing the biggest, best party (remember the water turned into wine?), and everyone is invited: all you have to do is come.

But, the story goes, the people that you'd expect to come to the party, instead didn't want to go. One after another, they kept making excuses. "I'm sorry, I'm much too busy to take time off this week," said one. "I just bought some new stuff, and I'd rather play with it," said another. "No thanks," said a third. "My family and friends are more important to me than your party." Which is totally ridiculous: when a king throws a party, you know it's going to be awesome. And if the king invites you, you'd better show up, because it's an insult to the king to turn up your nose at his invitation. But these people all thought they had "better things to do" than go to the king's party.

When the king heard that no one wanted to come to his party, he was angry. The reason he was angry was that it was obvious that all these people didn't really care about the king at all. So instead, the king went out, and found all the beggars and poor people and sick people. "They'll appreciate my party," the king said. And they did—it was better than anything they could ever have imagined or hoped for. But the end of the story is sad: all the people who were originally invited to the party, but didn't want to go, found themselves on the outside, wishing they could get in. But now it was too late.

Remember, this story is about Jesus and the invitation to be a part of his kingdom and enjoy his party forever. The invitation goes to everyone. In fact, did you know that you're invited? That's right: Jesus wants you to be a part of his kingdom. He wants you at his party. The way to accept his invitation and get into the party is to simply come to him: to come saying you're sorry for the things you've done wrong, knowing that you can't earn anything from Jesus, asking him to forgive you. For people who come empty-handed like that, the door to heaven is wide open. And you'll get to join the party that lasts into eternity and gets better and better every day forever.

But if you decide that you're too busy for Jesus, or that Jesus is okay but all the other stuff you love is a lot better, or you're just not really impressed by Jesus or his invitation, the ending of your story is sad: the door to the party is closed. Jesus doesn't let people into his heavenly party who don't care about him, who don't come to him for forgiveness, who don't want to be part of his kingdom.

So which of the people in the story are you going to be like? The people who made excuses, and got shut out? Or the poor people who didn't have anything, and got to come in and enjoy the never-ending party? Don't be one of the people who make excuses because they love stuff more. The door is open, the invitation has your name on it: but you have to come to Jesus if you want to go in.

Thanksgiving is about Jesus

Now on his way to Jerusalem, Jesus traveled along the border between Samaria and Galilee. As he was going into a village, ten men who had leprosy met him. They stood at a distance and called out in a loud voice, "Jesus, Master, have pity on us!" When he saw them, he said, "Go, show yourselves to the priests." And as they went, they were cleansed.
One of them, when he saw he was healed, came back, praising God in a loud voice. He threw himself at Jesus' feet and thanked him—and he was a Samaritan.
Jesus asked, "Were not all ten cleansed? Where are the other nine? Has no one returned to give praise to God except this foreigner?" Then he said to him, "Rise and go; your faith has made you well." –Luke 17:11-19

Think about all we've seen and learned about Jesus so far. He's the Life of the party, the good King who is in the process of undoing all sadness and death and sin, and who invites us to join his kingdom celebration. He's the Bread of life, who multiplies food out of thin air, the only One who can fill us up with happiness forever. He has compassion on lepers; he loves the unlovable, touches the untouchable, forgives the unforgivable. He is the God who rules over every wind and wave, and walks on the water just to prove to his friends that he is there to take care of them. He's gentle and powerful, raising the dead and befriending the worst people, all because he is a Savior who came to seek and save the lost. He loves being interrupted, loves forgiving sin, and loves celebrating when sinners come home.

What's the right response to a King like this? How should we respond to how wonderful and good and kind and strong and loving Jesus is? The way we should respond is: thanksgiving. If you know and love Jesus—if he has forgiven all your sin, made you God's child, and brought you into the kingdom party that lasts forever—you should be overflowing with thankfulness for how wonderful he has been to you. So why is that, so often, we don't thank him?

That's the point of this story. Ten lepers—remember how gross and terrible leprosy is?—begged Jesus to heal them, and because Jesus loves gross people, he gladly healed them. They all ran away, happy to be free of the terrible disease. Jesus had made them better, and they couldn't wait to get their lives back, and go home to their friends and family. But one leper turned around. I'm sure he wanted to go home too, but at that moment one person was way more important to him than all his other friends and family. He wanted to go back to Jesus.

He fell down at Jesus' feet, overwhelmed with thankfulness. He was so glad, so amazed that Jesus had took pity on him, so in awe of how great and wonderful Jesus was, that he just wanted to stay there forever, thanking Jesus over and over again.

You see, that one leper understood what the other nine didn't. They had gotten their healing and were happy about it, I'm sure. But they missed the main thing: that all the miracles, all the healings, are all about Jesus: they're to show us how wonderful he is, and make our hearts overflow with thankfulness.

So think about all the ways that Jesus has been kind to you. You have a family and a home and friends and toys and a million blessings. But far more than that, you have a Savior who loves you, who went to the cross to forgive you, who invites you into his never-ending party.

So how thankful are you?

stinky shepherds

And there were shepherds living out in the fields nearby, keeping watch over their flocks at night. An angel of the Lord appeared to them, and the glory of the Lord shone around them, and they were terrified. But the angel said to them, "Do not be afraid. I bring you good news that will cause great joy for all the people. Today in the town of David a Savior has been born to you; he is the Messiah, the Lord. This will be a sign to you: You will find a baby wrapped in cloths and lying in a manger."

Suddenly a great company of the heavenly host appeared with the angel, praising God and saying, "Glory to God in the highest heaven, and on earth peace to those on whom his favor rests."

When the angels had left them and gone into heaven, the shepherds said to one another, "Let's go to Bethlehem and see this thing that has happened, which the Lord has told us about."

So they hurried off and found Mary and Joseph, and the baby, who was lying in the manger. When they had seen him, they spread the word concerning what had been told them about this child, and all who heard it were amazed at what the shepherds said to them. But Mary treasured up

all these things and pondered them in her heart. The shepherds returned, glorifying and praising God for all the things they had heard and seen, which were just as they had been told.
–Luke 2:8-20

Do you have a nativity set at home that your family puts out around Christmas time? Take a look at it sometime, and think about just how strange and wonderful and surprising that little scene is.

If you were the King of the world about to start your long-planned rescue mission, how would you do it? March in with a big army? Ride on a white horse, with shining armor and servants and trumpets blaring? Would you go on all the TV news stations and announce your plans? Would you plaster it all over ther internet so that everyone would know? Would you gather all the presidents and prime ministers and kings and generals and make them do whatever you said?

King Jesus, the greatest king who has ever lived, arriving on the greatest rescue mission the world has ever seen, did none of those things. The rescue mission started with one angel bringing some news to one young girl in a small town in an obscure part of the world that nobody cared about. And when Jesus was born that first Christmas night, the news wasn't announced to kings and presidents. It was announced to the last people you would have ever thought: stinky shepherds.

That's right, shepherds. Back in Bible times,

shepherds were kind of like garbage collectors today. It was an important job, but it was a lowly, smelly job that most people didn't want. Nobody ever said, "I want to be a shepherd when I grow up." Being a shepherd was a job you got made fun of for having. Shepherds were rough around the edges, not the kind of people you would invite to nice parties.

But these were the people that God wanted at his Son's birthday party. When the angel announced to the shepherds, "Today a Savior has been born *for you*," he meant, "For you stinky shepherds, and everyone else that nobody cares about." That's why the next thing the angel said was, "Here's a sign for you shepherds: the promised King isn't in a palace. You'll find him in a stable, in a manger. He's poor, just like you."

The shepherds couldn't believe their ears. God had sent his Son, the promised King... for *them*? And sure enough, they found the baby just like the angels had said. He wasn't dressed in royal robes; he was wrapped in swaddling clothes, just like any other poor baby in the not-so-nice side of town. He wasn't in a palace; he was in a stable... just like the stables the shepherds probably had at their own houses. The promised king even *smelled* kind of like a shepherd, laying there in that feeding trough surrounded by animals.

That's because this King hadn't come to have servants and armies and to sit on a throne. He had come to *be* a servant, to love the forgotten and the nobodies, and to give his life away for people just like these stinky shepherds.

The Backwards, Upside-Down King

God sent the angel Gabriel to Nazareth, a town in Galilee, to a virgin pledged to be married to a man named Joseph, a descendant of David. The virgin's name was Mary. The angel went to her and said, "Greetings, you who are highly favored! The Lord is with you."

Mary was greatly troubled at his words and wondered what kind of greeting this might be. But the angel said to her, "Do not be afraid, Mary; you have found favor with God. You will conceive and give birth to a son, and you are to call him Jesus. He will be great and will be called the Son of the Most High. The Lord God will give him the throne of his father David, and he will reign over Jacob's descendants forever; his kingdom will never end."

"How will this be," Mary asked the angel, "since I am a virgin?"

The angel answered, "The Holy Spirit will come on you, and the power of the Most High will overshadow you. So the holy one to be born will be called the Son of God. Even Elizabeth your relative is going to have a child in her old age, and she who was said to be unable to conceive is in her sixth month. For no word from God will ever fail."

"I am the Lord's servant," Mary answered. "May your word to me be fulfilled." Then the angel left her. –Luke 1:26-38

Look at the baby in the manger—tiny, helpless, crying, covered in straw and a little bit of animal poop—and then listen again to the words that the angel said to Mary, and see if they fit with what you see in that manger:

"He will be great, and will be called the Son of the Most High. The Lord God will give him the throne of his father David, and he will reign over Jacob's descendants forever; his kingdom will never end."

Does this little baby look "great?" Does he look like what you'd expect the Son of the Most High God to look like? Does he look like the promised King who will reign forever?

No? That's because God loves to surprise us, to do things we'd never expect, things that seem upside-down and backwards. Upside-down, backwards things like leaving heaven's throne to become poor, like the King of kings being born as a baby, like announcing his birth to shepherds. Upside-down, backwards things like touching gross lepers, like loving unlovable sinners, like welcoming little creeps like Zacchaeus. Upside-down, backwards things like loving his enemies, like going to the cross to the pay for rebels' sins, like dying in order to beat death.

Christmas is the story of God doing all sorts of upside-down, backwards things. Actually, scratch that; that's not quite right: God's not actually the one who's upside-down and backwards. *We're* the ones who are upside-down and backwards, not God. It's like if you stand on your head, everything looks upside-down, but of course it's not really; you're actually the one who's upside-down. We've got everything backwards: we put ourselves first instead of other people, we obey our own thoughts instead of God's, we think that being tough and strong and smart and beautiful and good is the way to be special (instead of what God says: that being humble and gentle and a servant and sorry for your sins is the only way to be special in his kingdom).

And so when King Jesus shows up doing things the right way—putting other people before himself, being humble and kind and gentle and patient, serving others, and sacrificing himself even for his enemies—it may look upside-down to us, but it's not really. This is the way things are supposed to look like. This whole time, we've been the ones who are upside-down.

So it turns out that Christmas isn't the story of God doing upside-down things, after all. Instead, Christmas is the story of God starting to put everything right-ways up again. It's the beginning of the great reversal, of sins being forgiven and sinners being restored and everything sad coming untrue.

So look at that baby in the manger again. He really is great, because what greatness really looks like is humility. He really is the King of kings, because God's true King came not to be served but to serve, and to give his life as a ransom for many. This little baby is putting everything right-ways up again.

The Missing Nativity Piece

When Herod realized that he had been outwitted by the wise men, he was furious, and he gave orders to kill all the boys in Bethlehem and its vicinity who were two years old and under, in accordance with the time he had learned from the Magi. Then what was said through the prophet Jeremiah was fulfilled:
"A voice is heard in Ramah, weeping and great mourning, Rachel weeping for her children and refusing to be comforted, because they are no more." –Matthew 2:16-18

Look at all the pieces of your Nativity set sometime. There's Mary and Joseph, and baby Jesus of course (can't forget him!), some shepherds, perhaps an angel, probably some animals, and then there are those wise men. (Of course, the wise men didn't get there until a little later, but that's okay; they come with presents, which means they're kind of Christmassy, so I guess they can stay). If your Nativity set is extra fancy, you might even have a stable or a star.

Are you missing any pieces of the Christmas story? What about the soldiers?

"The soldiers?" you might ask. You probably don't remember seeing soldiers on any Christmas cards. But the soldiers are actually an important part of the Christmas story, only we usually forget about them because they don't go very well with our nice, sweet "silent night," "peace on earth" view of Christmas.

You see, the Christmas story doesn't end with the angels or the shepherds, or even the wise men coming to visit Jesus. The Christmas story actually ends with something terrible, one of the most terrible things in the Bible: King Herod, angry that the wise men didn't hand Jesus over to him, sends his soldiers on a murderous rampage and kills every single little boy in Bethlehem.

That's terrible—I don't even want to think about it that much because I might cry (after all, I have a little boy, just the right age to have been killed in Bethlehem). That horrible violence certainly doesn't fit on any of our Christmas cards. But it's a really important part of the Christmas story. Because without it, our Christmas runs the risk of being so cheesy— "away in the manger," "peace on earth," snow and mangers and presents—that we might never really have to think about *why* Jesus came in the first place.

Jesus came because our world is really, really messed up. People do bad things to each other. Terrible things happen, sometimes accidentally and sometimes on purpose. People get hurt, people die, people cry. Our whole world is filled with hurt and death and tears. Ever since Satan tricked Adam and Eve to try life without God, Satan has been doing his very best to make hell on earth.

So, when the angels announced, "Peace on earth," they weren't just singing a sweet song. It was God declaring war: war on Satan, war on sin and suffering and crying and pain and death. Christmas is the violent beginning to a violent war story: which side will win? Hell on earth, or peace on earth?

The story starts with blood and tears on Christmas, and keeps going right up to the blood and tears of Good Friday. It will take the death of this Savior to beat the power of sin and death and hell. But the story doesn't end there: the empty tomb of Easter proves that on that dark Friday, Jesus won; that even today, Jesus is winning; and that one day, Jesus will win.

A few years ago, I was at a Christmas eve service when an elderly gentleman had a heart attack, right in the middle of us singing "Joy to the World." It was kind of shocking (don't worry, though; the ambulance came and he ended up being okay), but it was a reminder of this truth: that "peace on earth" isn't here yet. I went home that night and wrote a poem about it. I called it, "Christmas is an Act of War."

While singing songs one holy night
About the birth of love's pure light,
I felt more deeply than before:
Christmas is an act of war

The baby in a manger came
As conqueror, to end sin's reign
God invaded Satan's shore;
Christmas is an act of war

Amidst our brokenness and pain,
Curse and fall and evil's reign
He comes to spread His blessings far;
Christmas is an act of war

He appeared to take our sin
The curse undo and victory win
The devil's work to full destroy
And vanquish grief with vaulted joy

So joyful and triumphant sing,
Battle hymns then let us ring
Insurrection anthems pour;
For Christmas is an act of war

Joy to all the world we sing,
Glory to the newborn King
Christ the Victor come adore
For Christmas is an act of war

The Christmas story—the whole Christmas story, with the soldiers and everything—is a reminder that even though the victory has been won, the war isn't over yet. People still hurt, hearts still break, bad things still happen. But not always. Not forever. That baby in the manger came as conqueror, crushed Satan at the cross, and is coming back one day to finish the job. "Peace on earth" will win.

King of Kings

After Jesus was born in Bethlehem in Judea, during the time of King Herod, Magi from the east came to Jerusalem and asked, "Where is the one who has been born king of the Jews? We saw his star when it rose and have come to worship him." When King Herod heard this he was disturbed, and all Jerusalem with him. When he had called together all the people's chief priests and teachers of the law, he asked them where the Messiah was to be born. "In Bethlehem in Judea," they replied, "for this is what the prophet has written:

"'But you, Bethlehem, in the land of Judah, are by no means least among the rulers of Judah; for out of you will come a ruler who will shepherd my people Israel.'"

Then Herod called the Magi secretly and found out from them the exact time the star had appeared. He sent them to Bethlehem and said, "Go and search carefully for the child. As soon as you find him, report to me, so that I too may go and worship him."

After they had heard the king, they went on their way, and the star they had seen when it rose went ahead of them until it stopped over the place where the child was. When they saw the star, they were overjoyed. On coming to the house, they saw the child with his mother Mary, and they bowed down and worshiped him. Then they opened their treasures and presented him with gifts of gold, frankincense and myrrh. And having been warned in a dream not to go back to Herod, they returned to their country by another route. –Matthew 2:1-12

When you read the gospel of Matthew, there's one really important theme that keeps getting hammered on over and over again: that Jesus is the true King, the King of Israel, the King of all kings. That's why Matthew puts this story about the wise men right after the Christmas story: so that, just in case we had missed it, we would know that this little baby is the King of the whole world.

Just think about it: these royal-looking wise men coming from a distant land, bearing kingly presents with them. When they first arrive, they come to Jerusalem, the capital (because they figure that's where a king would be), and start asking to see the newborn king. The authorities in Jerusalem point them to an ancient Old Testament prophecy that said the long-promised King would come from Bethlehem. So the royal visitors march down to the royal city of Bethlehem to pay a royal visit to the royal baby. Everything about this story shouts, "This is him! This is the King!"

And this King, who had come in such an unexpected, upside-down way, was even more amazing than anybody at the time realized. People at the time were expecting a King who would rule Israel, like King David of old. But King Jesus had come to do far more than that; he had come to be the King of the whole world. People from every nation all over the earth would bow down to him; people from every language would sing his praise. And one day, even those who hated him will be forced to bow, and every person who has ever lived will proclaim, "Jesus Christ is Lord!"

That's a big deal. That's how great King Jesus is. So look again at these foreign wise men, with their strange language and their funny clothes, bowing down to the baby King. This is a picture of what Jesus had come to be: the King over every nation, the King above all kings.

And now here we are, 2,000 years later, on the other side of the world from Bethlehem, and we can see God's promise coming true. King Jesus is worshipped and loved and obeyed here, and all around the world. He is still the King over every president and every king.

But there are some places, some nations, who still

haven't heard about him. They haven't heard the news of how the great King has come to save them. They're still lost in their sins, and Jesus has given us the job of taking the good news of his reign to them, so that they would join his kingdom party too, until his kingdom reaches around the whole world.

You can't sit on the Fence

When the time came for the purification rites required by the Law of Moses, Joseph and Mary took him to Jerusalem to present him to the Lord (as it is written in the Law of the Lord, "Every firstborn male is to be consecrated to the Lord"), and to offer a sacrifice in keeping with what is said in the Law of the Lord: "a pair of doves or two young pigeons."
Now there was a man in Jerusalem called Simeon, who was righteous and devout. He was waiting for the consolation of Israel, and the Holy Spirit was on him. It had been revealed to him by the Holy Spirit that he would not die before he had seen the Lord's Messiah. Moved by the Spirit, he went into the temple courts. When the parents brought in the child Jesus to do for him what the custom of the Law required, Simeon took him in his arms and praised God, saying:
"Sovereign Lord, as you have promised, you may now dismiss your servant in peace. For my eyes have seen your salvation, which you have prepared in the sight of all nations: a light for revelation to the Gentiles, and the glory of your people Israel."
The child's father and mother marveled at what

was said about him. Then Simeon blessed them and said to Mary, his mother: "This child is destined to cause the falling and rising of many in Israel, and to be a sign that will be spoken against, so that the thoughts of many hearts will be revealed. And a sword will pierce your own soul too." –Luke 2:22-35

There's one more story about baby Jesus that we have to look at together, and this one is just a little bit scary. It's not that the story itself is scary—I mean, after all, Jesus is just a baby, and how scary can a baby really be? Rather, it's something that's said about Jesus in the story—something that, if it's really true, should make us a little nervous about this baby.

When Jesus was just a baby, Mary and Joseph brought him on his first trip to the temple in Jerusalem. While they were there, they met an old man named Simeon, who was waiting there to see the Messiah, God's chosen King. When he saw baby Jesus, the Holy Spirit whispered to his heart, "Here's the King!" Simeon was so happy that he had lived to see the day when God's salvation finally arrived. He praised God for letting him see the promised Savior, and then he turned to Mary.

"This baby," he said to Mary, "will be like a fork in the road to everyone who meets him; they will go one way or the other. No one will be able to stay on the fence about him; they will either follow him, or they will fall away from him. He will make everyone choose sides."

If you stop and think about it for a minute, that's kind of a scary thing to say about this Savior. Sometimes we like to think of Jesus as so gentle and kind that nothing bad could ever happen because of him. But Simeon said that there was something about Jesus that would make everyone choose sides, and many people would choose the wrong side. Some people would meet Jesus and love him. Others would meet Jesus and hate him. But nobody could sit on the fence and just be like, "Oh, Jesus, he's okay I guess."

What makes this story kind of scary is that that's exactly what a lot of people try to do today. They try to say, "Oh Jesus, he's cool. I'll sing songs on Sunday, and I'll learn about him in chapel or whatever, but he's not that big of a deal to me. He's okay I guess. But I really love other stuff."

But what Simeon said is still true: you can't stay on the fence about Jesus. Either you believe he really is the King, he really is the Savior, he really did conquer death, and that changes everything… or he's a nobody, and you should stop paying attention. There isn't any middle ground that makes sense. Either he's the King, or he's a clown. Either he's the Way, the Truth, and the Life… or he's a liar and a loser.

So you can either fall down and worship him, or walk away. You can believe him, or not. You can give him your heart and your life and follow him forever, or you can throw him out and go on with your life. But the one thing you can't do is have it both ways: you can't sorta like Jesus, but not really be into following him. He didn't leave that option open. You've got to get off the fence.

God Growing Up

Every year Jesus' parents went to Jerusalem for the Festival of the Passover. When he was twelve years old, they went up to the festival, according to the custom. After the festival was over, while his parents were returning home, the boy Jesus stayed behind in Jerusalem, but they were unaware of it. Thinking he was in their company, they traveled on for a day. Then they began looking for him among their relatives and friends. When they did not find him, they went back to Jerusalem to look for him. After three days they found him in the temple courts, sitting among the teachers, listening to them and asking them questions. Everyone who heard him was amazed at his understanding and his answers. When his parents saw him, they were astonished. His mother said to him, "Son, why have you treated us like this? Your father and I have been anxiously searching for you."

"Why were you searching for me?" he asked. "Didn't you know I had to be in my Father's house?" But they did not understand what he was saying to them.

Then he went down to Nazareth with them and was obedient to them. But his mother treasured all these things in her heart. And Jesus grew in wisdom and stature, and in favor with God and man. –Luke 2:41-52

Have you ever wondered what Jesus was like growing up? Jesus is God himself come to live with us as a person. And God knows everything, and is all-powerful, and perfectly holy. But even though Jesus is God, he is also fully human—a perfect human, but human nonetheless. He got tired, he had to eat. As a baby he had poopy diapers. He learned to talk, just like you did when you were little.

So what does it look like to be fully God and fully man? What did God act like as a toddler? (I have a two-year-old at home; I am willing to bet that Jesus was *much* better behaved than him). What was God's first day of school like? Did Jesus have to learn anything as a kid, or did he already know everything because he was God? What would it have been like to have Jesus in your class? Or for him to be your older brother? To be honest, I'm not quite sure what the answers to those questions are.

I kind of wish the Bible told us more (because I'm curious!), but we only have one story of Jesus as a kid. The reason we only have one story is because it was what Jesus did when he grew up that is really important for us, not what he did as a boy. But we do have this one glimpse of Jesus as a twelve-year-old. This is Jesus as a sixth-grader. If you've ever wondered what a perfect sixth-grader looks like, this is it. And it's not quite what you would expect.

It's actually kind of a funny story. Jesus' family went on their annual family vacation to Jerusalem, to celebrate Passover (maybe you go to the beach every year; Jesus' family went to Jerusalem). While they were there, Jesus' mom and dad accidently misplaced Jesus. Maybe dad thought he was with mom, or mom thought he was with dad, or they both thought he was with the cousins from Nazareth. They were halfway home before they realized he wasn't with them. (Can you imagine how they must have felt? They lost God! Whoops!)

So where had Jesus wandered off to? The toy store? The movies? The football game? The mall? Maybe that's where you would wander off to, because you really love those things, but Jesus loved something else much more. He went to his heavenly Father's house, the temple. Because even as a boy, what Jesus loved more than anything was his heavenly Father (that, by the way, is exactly what it means to be perfect: to love God more than anything else).

When Mary and Joseph finally tracked down

Jesus, they found him in the temple asking all the religious leaders brilliant, probing questions. All the religious leaders were amazed by this kid. He asked questions they didn't have answers to, and it seemed like he wasn't asking just because he was curious, but because he somehow know the answers already. It almost seemed like this sixth-grade kid was trying to teach *them*. They had never met someone like this before.

When Mary and Joseph, flustered and exasperated, asked Jesus why he hadn't gone home with them, he answered, "Didn't you know I'd be here, in my Father's house?" like it was the most obvious thing in the world. And it should have been obvious: Jesus loved his Father more than anything in the world. Where else, after all, would he want to be?

Taking the Test For You, Part 1

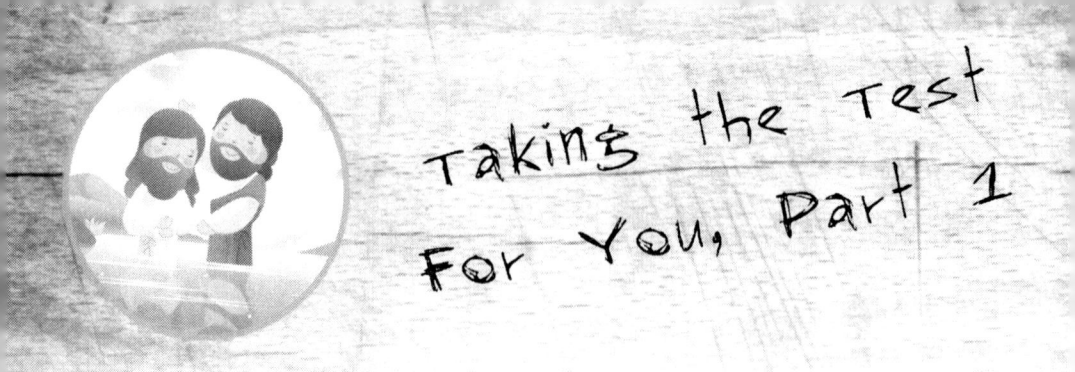

Then Jesus came from Galilee to the Jordan to be baptized by John. But John tried to deter him, saying, "I need to be baptized by you, and do you come to me?"
Jesus replied, "Let it be so now; it is proper for us to do this to fulfill all righteousness." Then John consented.
As soon as Jesus was baptized, he went up out of the water. At that moment heaven was opened, and he saw the Spirit of God descending like a dove and alighting on him. And a voice from heaven said, "This is my Son, whom I love; with him I am well pleased." –Matthew 3:13-17

Before Jesus started working miracles, before he began calling disciples, before he started preaching, Jesus first went down to the river to be baptized. People from all over were coming to John the Baptist to be baptized as a sign that they were sorry for their sins and wanted to obey God now. Jesus, of course, had never sinned even once, so he had no sins to be sorry for. That's why John the Baptist was so surprised to see him there. "I need to be baptized by you!" John protested. But Jesus insisted; he wanted to be baptized too.

Jesus insisted on being baptized, even though he didn't have any sins to be sorry for, for a very important reason: Jesus didn't just come to pay the debt for all the bad things we've done; he also came to do all the good things we haven't done. On the cross, Jesus paid the punishment for every sin you've ever committed: every time you were angry, every time you were selfish, every time you told a lie, every time you loved something else more than God. He paid the price for all of them, in your place on the cross, so that you could be forgiven.

But Jesus also did more than that: he also did all the good things you haven't done, in your place, so that all the good things he did could count for you. He loved people perfectly, and trusted his Father perfectly, and obeyed perfectly—everything we haven't done, even though we're supposed to. So if you trust Jesus, God doesn't look at you and see all the ways you fail; he looks at you and sees all the ways Jesus succeeded, and treats you as if you did all those good things. It's as if your teacher gave you a test, and you failed miserably—like, epic fail—and got every single question wrong. But Jesus got 100% on the test, and wrote your name on his test, so that his perfect grade could count for you.

We don't love people like we should; but Jesus loved people perfectly in our place, so that God can be happy with us anyway. We don't trust God very much; Jesus trusted his Father perfectly in our place, so that God could reward even our tiny faith. We only obey God halfheartedly (if at all), but Jesus did obey perfectly in our place, so that God can rejoice over us just like he rejoices over Jesus. We're not even sorry for our sins the way we should be; but Jesus went to be baptized and repent in our place, so that God can still forgive us even though we could never be sorry enough.

All the good things Jesus did can count for you; you can have his 100% grade. You don't have to earn it (as if you could even try!). You don't have to be "good enough" (because Jesus was already "good enough" for you!). The free gift of forgiveness and a perfect grade with God is just that: a free gift. All you have to do is ask for it.

Taking the Test For You, Part 2

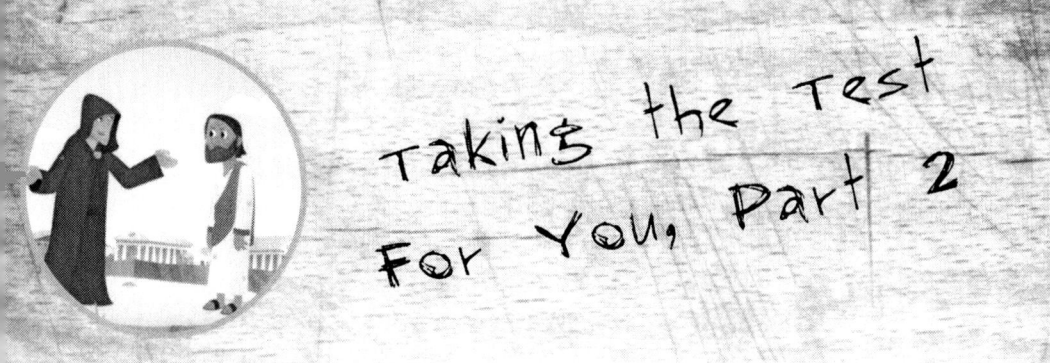

Then Jesus was led by the Spirit into the wilderness to be tempted by the devil. After fasting forty days and forty nights, he was hungry. The tempter came to him and said, "If you are the Son of God, tell these stones to become bread."
Jesus answered, "It is written: 'Man shall not live on bread alone, but on every word that comes from the mouth of God.'"
Then the devil took him to the holy city and had him stand on the highest point of the temple. "If you are the Son of God," he said, "throw yourself down. For it is written:
"'He will command his angels concerning you, and they will lift you up in their hands, so that you will not strike your foot against a stone.'"
Jesus answered him, "It is also written: 'Do not put the Lord your God to the test.'"
Again, the devil took him to a very high mountain and showed him all the kingdoms of the world and their splendor. "All this I will give you," he said, "if you will bow down and worship me."
Jesus said to him, "Away from me, Satan! For it is written: 'Worship the Lord your God, and serve him only.'"
Then the devil left him, and angels came and attended him. –Matthew 4:1-11

The very next thing that happened after Jesus' baptism was not what you'd expect. Instead of immediately marching into town to start preaching and healing people, instead Jesus marched out into the desert. He stayed there for 40 days without eating anything. Just think of how weak and hungry he must have been (I can hardly go 40 minutes without food, let alone 40 days)!

Then, when Jesus must have been close to collapsing, it got worse: the devil showed up. He had been waiting for a moment of weakness, and now he pounced. Satan knew that if he could trick Jesus, get him to mess up here, the whole rescue mission would be off. Jesus had to be perfect, so that he could earn that 100% grade for us and then be a perfect sacrifice for our sins. A 99% wouldn't be good enough. So all that Satan needed was one little slip up. Satan probably thought it would be easy; after all, he had convinced Adam and Eve to eat the forbidden fruit even when they had all the other food they could want. Every day, Satan finds it easy to trick you and me into loving stuff more than we love God. And now Jesus was starving; convincing him to make himself some lunch should be no trouble at all. But Satan underestimated just how dedicated Jesus was to obeying God and God alone.

You might wonder what's so bad about these temptations that Satan used on Jesus. After all, there's nothing wrong with turning rocks into bread, is there? But Satan is sneaky; all of his temptations of Jesus were really about the same thing: trying to get Jesus to stop trusting his Father's plan, and to use his power to help himself. Satan was saying, "You're a miracle worker, aren't you? Use some of that power to help yourself for once! You want a big crowd to follow you? Just do this neat trick, and then everyone will believe you! You want people from all nations to follow you? I'll make them do it, as long as you do it my way."

But each time, Jesus stood firm. Each time Satan offered him the easy way out, Jesus chose the hard way instead. He loved and trusted his Father. He obeyed, no matter the cost. He was determined to earn that 100% grade—not for himself, but for you.

That's right—this test wasn't just for himself; it was for you too. Every time you've given into temptation, Jesus succeeded. Every time you disobeyed, Jesus obeyed. And he did it all so that his perfect grade could count for you, so that he could write your name at the top of his test and you get all the credit.

You need a 100% grade to get into heaven; God is so perfect and holy that he won't accept anything less. So thank God that Jesus succeeded where we failed. Our only hope is his 100% grade. And because he aced the test, the doors of heaven are open to failures like us.

Here comes the Kingdom

When Jesus heard that John had been put in prison, he withdrew to Galilee. Leaving Nazareth, he went and lived in Capernaum, which was by the lake in the area of Zebulun and Naphtali— to fulfill what was said through the prophet Isaiah: "Land of Zebulun and land of Naphtali, the Way of the Sea, beyond the Jordan, Galilee of the Gentiles — the people living in darkness have seen a great light; on those living in the land of the shadow of death a light has dawned."
From that time on Jesus began to preach, "Repent, for the kingdom of heaven has come near." – Matthew 4:12-17

After Jesus' first miracle—taking a lame party and making it awesome, remember?—he began travelling around from town to town preaching. What was he preaching about? To put it simply: he was inviting everyone to the kingdom party.

Except that there was a problem. Remember how Jesus told that story about how the king invited everyone to his party, and no one wanted to come? Well, that story is kind of what we're like, and it's what the people who heard Jesus were like too. Jesus was announcing the coming of God's kingdom—the celebration of life and peace and mercy and joy that lasts forever—but most people couldn't be bothered. They were too busy with their lives, too impressed with their own importance, too puffed up with their own goodness—to pay much attention to the invitation.

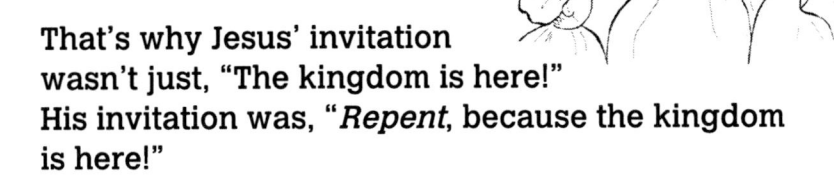

That's why Jesus' invitation wasn't just, "The kingdom is here!" His invitation was, "*Repent*, because the kingdom is here!"

"Repent" might seem like a scary-sounding word, like somebody yelling at you to clean up your act. But the word "repent" simply means "turn around." You see, everyone in the whole world is running away from God—trying to be their own king, living for themselves, ignoring God—and what Jesus is saying is, "Stop running away from God! Turn around!" Because, obviously, you can't come into the party if you're running away from it. The only way to get into the party is to turn around—to give up trying to be your king and start following King Jesus instead. Once you turn around, you'll find that the door to the party is wide open, and you can come on in.

A famous, smart dead guy named Martin Luther once said, "The Christian life is a life of repentance." That means that following Jesus isn't just about turning around once. It means that every day is about turning around to follow Jesus. It means deciding again, every day, to not be your own king, and to follow Jesus again.

That sounds hard, and it is, but it's also the best thing in the world. Because, remember: this is an invitation to a party, the best party that's ever been thrown, by the greatest King the world has ever known. You're invited. All you have to do is turn around and come in.

A Lousy Bunch of Losers

Jesus went up on a mountainside and called to him those he wanted, and they came to him. He appointed twelve that they might be with him and that he might send them out to preach and to have authority to drive out demons. These are the twelve he appointed: Simon (to whom he gave the name Peter), James son of Zebedee and his brother John (to them he gave the name Boanerges, which means "sons of thunder"), Andrew, Philip, Bartholomew, Matthew, Thomas, James son of Alphaeus, Thaddaeus, Simon the Zealot and Judas Iscariot, who betrayed him. –Mark 3:13-19

Let's take a minute to get to know the strange band of characters that Jesus picked to be his closest friends. You can tell a lot about a person by looking to see who their friends are. And when you look at Jesus' friends… well, they certainly are characters. Let's meet a couple of them.

First up, there's Peter. His name means "rock," and not just because he was a dumb as a rock (which he kind of was). Well, it's not so much that he was dumb, but more that his heart was bigger than his brain. His mouth was always getting him into trouble, because he would always spout off the first thing that came into his head, even if it wasn't the wisest thing to say. And yet he really was bighearted; he was one of the first of Jesus' disciples to embrace who Jesus really was, and he loved Jesus fiercely. Even when he messed up (which he did, big time, repeatedly), he found Jesus welcoming him back.

Then there were the brothers James and John, whom Jesus nicknamed "Sons of Thunder," because, sort of like Peter, they were loud and strong— strong-hearted but also strong-headed. These guys were fisherman, which meant they were tough, and they were some of Jesus' closest friends. He loved their fire and their passion, even though that passion sometimes got them into trouble, like the time they decided that they were better than the other disciples and that they should get thrones right next to Jesus (eye roll, right?). Jesus set them straight in no uncertain terms: greatness in his kingdom, Jesus said, wasn't measured by how strong you were, but by how much you served others. Even though it took a while, they eventually got the message, and went on to spend the rest of their lives serving others and telling everyone how great Jesus was.

Next came Andrew. Andrew was one of the very first people to follow Jesus, and he loved telling people about him. In fact, he was the one who first brought his brother Peter to meet Jesus. Even though he wasn't as loud or talkative as some of the other disciples, it seems like Andrew really understood Jesus; he was the first to believe that Jesus was the promised King, the first to tell others about him, the first to understand what Jesus' miracles were about.

And then there was Thomas. Thomas was a pessimist, which meant he always saw the bad side of everything. He was like Eeyore, complaining about the weather and everything else too. He's only recorded saying three things in the gospels, and all of them were grumbling, complaining, and whining. But Jesus loved him anyway, and after Jesus' resurrection, Thomas' pessimism was turned upside-down, and he spent the rest of his life travelling all over the world telling people how Jesus was alive.

Matthew and Simon were polar opposites; they couldn't possibly be more different. Matthew had been a tax collector before he met Jesus, which means he had been a traitor who worked with the invading Romans to take people's money. Everyone hated tax collectors... well, everyone except Jesus. And Simon was a Zealot, which meant he was part of a group dedicated to overthrowing the Romans and kicking them out of Israel. That sounds like a good goal, except that the Zealots were violent and would kill anyone who got in their way. In fact, they were more like terrorists than anything else. So Jesus had picked a terrorist and a tax collector (which was the kind of person that a terrorist would like to kill), and made them both part of his team. These were two guys who used to hate each other more than anything else in the world... but Jesus brought them together and changed both their lives.

And finally, there was Judas, who would go on to betray Jesus (spoiler alert). And actually, he was more than a traitor; he was a thief, too. He was good with money and so the group had put him in charge of keeping all their money, but instead of keeping it safe, he would spend it on himself. Even though he spent three years with Jesus and saw all his miracles, in the end it turned out that he loved money more than he loved Jesus; when he had the opportunity, he ended up selling out Jesus for just thirty pieces of silver.

Can you believe that these were the friends that Jesus chose? Don't you think he should have chosen... well, *better* friends? This bumbling group of twelve knuckleheads were the last people you'd expect the King to pick to be his closest companions.

Except that this King was always picking the last people you'd expect. He was always loving the unlovable and forgiving the unforgivable, and hanging out with the sinners and the sick and the hurting. He had come to serve the least and the forgotten, the lowly and the losers. No wonder he picked these guys. And no wonder he loves people like you and me.

The Real celebrity

Jesus went through all the towns and villages, teaching in their synagogues, proclaiming the good news of the kingdom and healing every disease and sickness. When he saw the crowds, he had compassion on them, because they were harassed and helpless, like sheep without a shepherd. Then he said to his disciples, "The harvest is plentiful but the workers are few. Ask the Lord of the harvest, therefore, to send out workers into his harvest field." –Matthew 9:35-38

As Jesus travelled around from town to town preaching and healing, the word about him started to spread. More and more people showed up at each new town to hear this man talk—because he spoke like no one else they had ever heard—and to see him work miracles—because he did things no one else had ever done before. Jesus became more and more famous. Pretty soon everyone had heard of him, and everyone wanted to see him.

Have you ever had the chance to meet a famous person? Some celebrities are nice people, I'm sure, but more often than not, famous people can tend to be kind of self-centered and full of themselves. That's not because they're worse than you or me, but because there's something about fame and fortune that tends to make everybody selfish. I'm sure that if I suddenly became world famous, I would probably turn into a big jerk. The more people would think I was cool, the more I'd start to think that I was better than everyone else. That's how all our hearts are wired. Like a balloon filled with hot air, we get puffed up with pride really easily.

Which is why it's so surprising to see how Jesus responded to the crowds following him. He didn't sign autographs. He didn't come out for encore performances after each sermon. He didn't show off his miracles. In fact, the more famous he got, the more his heart seemed to break for the people following him. The attention didn't turn him self-centered; if anything, it seemed to make him care about people even more.

He looked out over the crowds of people, and he didn't think about how great he was (and remember, unlike our celebrities, Jesus really was great!) Instead, he saw each person individually. He saw their hurts and their fears and their sins. His heart broke for all the hurting people crowding around him. He knew that they were like poor defenseless sheep without a shepherd to keep them safe and well. He had come to be their

Good Shepherd, to be Savior to the lost and hurting, because he loved them. He felt the great weight of all their hurts and needs. That's why he said to his disciples, "The harvest is plentiful but the laborers are few. Pray for God to send out more laborers."

He saw the hurt everywhere, and he knew it would take many, many people to take the news of his rescue to everyone who needed to hear it.

That's the kind of celebrity Jesus was, and is today. He still loves hurting, broken people. He still loves to forgive sinners, and welcome back the lost. And he's still sending people like you and me to go and find them and bring them home.

The Bad Guys

To some who were confident of their own righteousness and looked down on everyone else, Jesus told this parable: "Two men went up to the temple to pray, one a Pharisee and the other a tax collector. The Pharisee stood by himself and prayed: 'God, I thank you that I am not like other people—robbers, evildoers, adulterers—or even like this tax collector. I fast twice a week and give a tenth of all I get.'

"But the tax collector stood at a distance. He would not even look up to heaven, but beat his breast and said, 'God, have mercy on me, a sinner.'

"I tell you that this man, rather than the other, went home justified before God. For all those who exalt themselves will be humbled, and those who humble themselves will be exalted." –Luke 18:9-14

Every good story needs a bad guy, and the story of Jesus is the best story in the history of the world. So of course it makes sense that we've got some great bad guys. The bad guys in Jesus' story were the Pharisees. But (and this is what makes them such good bad guys) they didn't seem like bad guys on the outside. In fact, most people would have thought they were the good guys. The

Pharisees were the people who were really serious about obeying God; they tried really hard to dress the right way, and eat the right way, and hang out with all the right people, and follow all the rules. That doesn't sound bad, right? So what was so bad about these Pharisees?

Well, just like a lot of things in the story of Jesus, we've got things upside-down and backwards. You see, the Pharisees thought that because they followed all the rules, that was what made them "good." In fact, they thought following all the rules made them better than everyone else. They didn't realize that you could follow all the rules on the outside, but still be arrogant and angry and hateful on the inside. People just saw their outsides—how good they seemed—and were impressed. But Jesus could see into their hearts, and he was not impressed. Over and over again, Jesus called them out on their hypocrisy (hypocrisy means acting good on the outside while being bad on the inside).

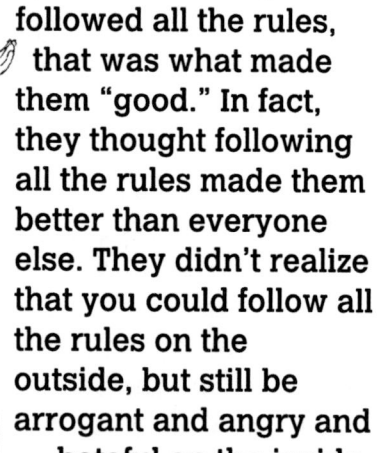

One time, Jesus told them a story to try to get them

to see how bad they really were. (Jesus wasn't trying to be mean; he was trying to help them, and show them how much they needed a Savior). He told them a story about a Pharisee who was so full of himself that even his prayers were braggy, and a tax collector (remember, tax collectors were traitors and everyone hated them). Unlike the Pharisee, this tax collector knew he was a sinner who needed a Savior. So, when the tax collector prayed, he wouldn't even lift his eyes to heaven. On his knees, with tears in his eyes, all he could pray was, "God, have mercy on me, a sinner."

When Jesus was done with his story, he looked the Pharisees right in the eye. "God accepted that tax collector, and rejected that Pharisee," he said. (People probably gasped when they heard that). "Because that tax collector knew he needed a Savior, and the only kind of people God saves are the ones who know they need saving."

Well, you can imagine how that went over with the Pharisees. They should have realized how wrong they were and begged for forgiveness like the tax collector. Instead, they got all offended. Who was this Jesus guy, they thought, to say all these mean things about them? Didn't he realize how awesome they were? He kept exposing them for the cheap phonies they were, and they hated it. And so, instead of humbling themselves and asking for mercy, they started plotting... plotting to get rid of Jesus.

The Future came Early

Now a man named Lazarus was sick. He was from Bethany, the village of Mary and her sister Martha. (This Mary, whose brother Lazarus now lay sick, was the same one who poured perfume on the Lord and wiped his feet with her hair.) So the sisters sent word to Jesus, "Lord, the one you love is sick."
When he heard this, Jesus said, "This sickness will not end in death. No, it is for God's glory so that God's Son may be glorified through it." Now Jesus loved Martha and her sister and Lazarus. So when he heard that Lazarus was sick, he stayed where he was two more days, and then he said to his disciples, "Let us go back to Judea..."
On his arrival, Jesus found that Lazarus had already been in the tomb for four days. Now Bethany was less than two miles from Jerusalem, and many Jews had come to Martha and Mary to comfort them in the loss of their brother. When Martha heard that Jesus was coming, she went out to meet him, but Mary stayed at home.
"Lord," Martha said to Jesus, "if you had been here, my brother would not have died. But I know that even now God will give you whatever you ask."
Jesus said to her, "Your brother will rise again."

Martha answered, "I know he will rise again in the resurrection at the last day."

Jesus said to her, "I am the resurrection and the life. The one who believes in me will live, even though they die; and whoever lives by believing in me will never die. Do you believe this?"

"Yes, Lord," she replied, "I believe that you are the Messiah, the Son of God, who is to come into the world."

After she had said this, she went back and called her sister Mary aside. "The Teacher is here," she said, "and is asking for you." When Mary heard this, she got up quickly and went to him. Now Jesus had not yet entered the village, but was still at the place where Martha had met him. When the Jews who had been with Mary in the house, comforting her, noticed how quickly she got up and went out, they followed her, supposing she was going to the tomb to mourn there.

When Mary reached the place where Jesus was and saw him, she fell at his feet and said, "Lord, if you had been here, my brother would not have died."

When Jesus saw her weeping, and the Jews who had come along with her also weeping, he was deeply moved in spirit and troubled. "Where have you laid him?" he asked.

"Come and see, Lord," they replied.

Jesus wept.

Then the Jews said, "See how he loved him!"

But some of them said, "Could not he who opened the eyes of the blind man have kept this man from dying?"

Jesus, once more deeply moved, came to the tomb.

It was a cave with a stone laid across the entrance. "Take away the stone," he said.
"But, Lord," said Martha, the sister of the dead man, "by this time there is a bad odor, for he has been there four days."
Then Jesus said, "Did I not tell you that if you believe, you will see the glory of God?"
So they took away the stone. Then Jesus looked up and said, "Father, I thank you that you have heard me. I knew that you always hear me, but I said this for the benefit of the people standing here, that they may believe that you sent me."
When he had said this, Jesus called in a loud voice, "Lazarus, come out!" The dead man came out, his hands and feet wrapped with strips of linen, and a cloth around his face.
Jesus said to them, "Take off the grave clothes and let him go." –John 11

Jesus loved everybody, but he also had friends who held a special place in his heart. Three of his closest friends were Lazarus and his sisters Mary and Martha. One day, Lazarus got sick... really sick. He was close to the point of death. But Mary and Martha weren't worried. They knew that as soon as Jesus heard, he would come and help them. He loved them, after all.

But Jesus did something shocking. When he got the news that Lazarus was dying, he didn't run down to their house right away. He waited. Actually, he waited several days. In fact, he waited so long that Lazarus died. Why in the world would Jesus do that? Didn't he love his friends?

Yes, he did—more than they knew. And in fact, even though they didn't understand it yet, he waited *because* he loved them, not in spite of it. That's what the story says: "Jesus loved Martha and her sister and Lazarus. *So,* when he heard that Lazarus was sick, he stayed where he was for two more days." He stayed *because* he loved them. He let Lazarus die *because* he loved them.

Why? That doesn't make any sense. If you love somebody, you want to help them, right? That's right, but in this case, Jesus wanted to help them with something even more important than healing their brother. He knew that the most important thing in the world was for them to understand who he really was. And so he waited until Lazarus had died, so that he could do something even more amazing than just healing him. He wanted them to not just see what he could do, but who he was.

By the time he got to Mary and Martha's house, Lazarus had been dead and buried for four days. Have you ever seen something that's been dead for a couple days—maybe a deer on the side of the road that got hit by a car? If so, you know that after four days, things start to get gross and smelly. Dead bodies start to decay pretty quickly. Jesus had raised dead people before—remember the little girl?—but nothing like this. Lazarus wasn't just mostly dead; he was full-blown dead-dead, rotting in the tomb. Nobody, not even Jesus, could fix this. Right?

Wrong.

When Jesus arrived, Martha came out to meet him and fell down at his feet weeping. "Jesus," she said, "If you had been here, my brother wouldn't have died."

"Your brother will rise again," Jesus responded.

Well, Mary knew that, but she thought Jesus was talking about heaven, and the final resurrection on the last day. "Yes, I know I'll see him in heaven one day, I know he'll rise in the resurrection at the last day," Mary responded. "A lot of good that does me now," she probably thought.

"Mary," Jesus said gently, "*I'm* the resurrection. *I'm* the life. Whoever believes in *me* will live forever, even if they die. Do you believe that?"

What he meant was, "Mary, don't just put your hope in some future event. That future event is *me*. *I'm* the resurrection. *I'm* the future you've been waiting for. The resurrection has arrived."

And just to back up that outrageous claim —to prove that he really was who he said he was—Jesus walked over to the dead man's stinky, rotting tomb, and called out, "Lazarus, come out!" And immediately, death started working backwards: the decay disappeared, cells knit themselves back together, brain and heart and muscles zapped to life, breath filled the dead man's lungs, and he came walking out of the tomb.

One day, this scene will happen all across the world. The Bible promises a day—the final day—when God will call every person who has ever lived out of their graves. Every dead person will rise. Graveyards will burst to life, dust will reassemble back into bodies, breath will fill long-gone lungs, and every human who has ever lived will live again and stand before God. God will remake the whole world to be a perfect home for his children and will roll back all decay and sin, and everyone who loves Jesus will live in the remade world with him forever.

That will happen one day. That's the future that God has promised. But for a little while, that future came early, in the person of Jesus. Wherever he went, that future came bursting in early, as death and decay and sin and sadness started working backwards and turning into life and beauty and hope and joy. He gave us a glimpse of what that future life will be, because he *is* that Life, the Life that lasts forever.

Here comes the King

The next day the great crowd that had come for the festival heard that Jesus was on his way to Jerusalem. They took palm branches and went out to meet him, shouting,
"Hosanna! Blessed is he who comes in the name of the Lord! Blessed is the king of Israel!"
Jesus found a young donkey and sat on it, as it is written:
"Do not be afraid, Daughter Zion; see, your king is coming, seated on a donkey's colt."
At first his disciples did not understand all this. Only after Jesus was glorified did they realize that these things had been written about him and that these things had been done to him.
Now the crowd that was with him when he called Lazarus from the tomb and raised him from the dead continued to spread the word. Many people, because they had heard that he had performed this sign, went out to meet him. So the Pharisees said to one another, "See, this is getting us nowhere. Look how the whole world has gone after him!" –John 12:12-19

The news about how Jesus had raised the really-really-super-dead Lazarus spread quickly, and everyone wanted to catch a glimpse of this great miracle worker. It was getting hard for Jesus to travel around freely, because all the crowds wanted to see him, and all the Pharisees wanted to kill him. Jesus knew that his time was almost up—events were starting to be put into motion that would end with him on the cross—but before that happened, he had a really important statement to make. But this wouldn't be a statement like a speech or a sermon. Jesus was going to *do* something, something that would speak much louder than words.

Jesus was on his way into Jerusalem, the capital city, and he knew that a huge crowd had gathered to see him. The crowds were sure that Jesus must be the long-awaited King, the King who would finally set them free and kick out all the bad guys and make everything good again. And in fact, Jesus was that King. But his plan was different from theirs. They wanted a king who would come riding in on a noble steed, dressed up in shiny armor, to do battle with the bad guys, to kick out those mean Romans. But Jesus had a much bigger, better plan: he had come to beat the worst enemy —sin and death and Satan—and to be the king of the whole world. But that was a victory that wouldn't come with guns or soldiers or armies. This was a victory that could only come by Jesus laying down his life.

Jesus knew that, but the people didn't. So, to show

them exactly what kind of king he was, Jesus arranged a ride. He didn't want to come riding in on a kingly horse, looking impressive, because people would get the wrong idea. Instead, Jesus picked the lowliest, humblest barnyard animal he could find: a donkey. Donkeys are slow. Donkeys are kind of silly-looking. So Jesus got on a donkey and started his march into Jerusalem.

Everyone was excited to see Jesus, but his mode of transportation probably raised a few eyebrows. You see, kings don't ride donkeys; servants ride donkeys. Poor people ride donkeys. Everyone was shouting, "Here comes the king! Praise the king!" And yet Jesus didn't look like a king, sitting there on that silly donkey. He looked... well, like a servant. Lowly. Humble.

Which was exactly the point. Jesus wanted to show them that he had come to be a humble king, the kind of king who helped others instead of being helped himself. The king of king who came to serve, not be served. The kind of king who came to give his life away to save his people.

And that's exactly what he was about to do.

A King Who Serves

It was just before the Passover Festival. Jesus knew that the hour had come for him to leave this world and go to the Father. Having loved his own who were in the world, he loved them to the end. The evening meal was in progress, and the devil had already prompted Judas, the son of Simon Iscariot, to betray Jesus. Jesus knew that the Father had put all things under his power, and that he had come from God and was returning to God; so he got up from the meal, took off his outer clothing, and wrapped a towel around his waist. After that, he poured water into a basin and began to wash his disciples' feet, drying them with the towel that was wrapped around him.
He came to Simon Peter, who said to him, "Lord, are you going to wash my feet?"
Jesus replied, "You do not realize now what I am doing, but later you will understand."
"No," said Peter, "you shall never wash my feet."
Jesus answered, "Unless I wash you, you have no part with me."
"Then, Lord," Simon Peter replied, "not just my feet but my hands and my head as well!"
Jesus answered, "Those who have had a bath need

only to wash their feet; their whole body is clean. And you are clean, though not every one of you." For he knew who was going to betray him, and that was why he said not every one was clean. When he had finished washing their feet, he put on his clothes and returned to his place. "Do you understand what I have done for you?" he asked them. "You call me 'Teacher' and 'Lord,' and rightly so, for that is what I am. Now that I, your Lord and Teacher, have washed your feet, you also should wash one another's feet. I have set you an example that you should do as I have done for you.
–John 13:1-15

Just a few days after Jesus rode into Jerusalem on a donkey to show he was the humble king coming to save his people, things were starting to move quickly. The crowds were beginning to figure out that Jesus wasn't the kind of king they had thought he was. The Pharisees had hatched a plot to get rid of Jesus, once and for all. They had convinced one of his friends, Judas, to betray Jesus. Everything was about to go down.

And Jesus knew all of this. It was all part of the plan, ever since before the beginning of time. This was the whole reason he had come: to die on the cross. But before that awful day, Jesus wanted one last dinner with his friends. He had important things to tell them, and even more important things to show them.

During dinner, Jesus got up from the table and took off his nice clothes. He tied a servant's apron around his waist, got a bowl of water and a towel, and got down on his knees and began to wash his friends' feet.

Now, there's something very important you have to know here. Today, we wear shoes and drive cars and spend more time inside, so our feet aren't usually that dirty (although maybe your feet smell sometimes). But back in Jesus' day, people wore sandals and walked around outside on dirt roads, where donkeys and horses and chickens were pooping. By the end of the day, their feet would be really gross—way more disgusting even than your feet after you've been running around outside. And so rich people would often have a slave whose job it was to wash their feet. It was such a dirty, smelly, embarrassing job that only the lowest slave would even think about doing it.

But here was Jesus, the King of all kings, God's own Son, with a servant's apron around his waist, doing the dirty job of a slave. Jesus' friends were shocked. Peter—big-hearted, small-brained Peter—was offended. "Heck no, Jesus!" he said angrily. "There's no way I'm going to let you do this." In Peter's mind, the King of kings should never do something this lowly.

But Jesus had an important lesson to teach them. "Do you understand what I've just done for you?" he asked his confused friends. "You call me Lord and Teacher and King... and you're right, that's exactly who I am. *But this is the kind of King I am.* I didn't come to be served, I came to serve, and to give my life away for you."

Jesus had come to do something way harder than clean feet; he came to clean hearts. And that was going to be ever messier job. That was going to take even more humility than being a servant; that was going to mean Jesus humbling himself all the way to death... death on a cross.

Scared Jesus

Jesus went out as usual to the Mount of Olives, and his disciples followed him. On reaching the place, he said to them, "Pray that you will not fall into temptation." He withdrew about a stone's throw beyond them, knelt down and prayed, "Father, if you are willing, take this cup from me; yet not my will, but yours be done." An angel from heaven appeared to him and strengthened him. And being in anguish, he prayed more earnestly, and his sweat was like drops of blood falling to the ground. When he rose from prayer and went back to the disciples, he found them asleep, exhausted from sorrow. "Why are you sleeping?" he asked them. "Get up and pray so that you will not fall into temptation." –Luke 22:39-46

After his final dinner with his disciples, Jesus went outside the city to a garden called Gethsemane. He had been there before; it was one of his favorite places to "get away" and pray. He had spent many hours talking with his Father there.

Jesus had come to this garden because he knew exactly what was about to happen; he knew that even as he prayed, Judas was gathering soldiers to come and arrest him. He knew that just a few hours from now, he would be beaten and nailed to the cross. He knew the pain and shame that was about to come down on him. And so he had come one last time to pray.

But this time, there was something different about Jesus. Something even a little scary. Up until this point, Jesus has always seemed "in charge," hasn't he? He speaks and weather obeys him. Demons tremble at him. Sickness and death run away when Jesus comes to town. He speaks and teaches like he's in charge, like no one else ever has. Even the Pharisees can't trick him, or trip him up, or stop him. Even when everything around him seems crazy, even when his disciples are freaking out, Jesus is like the calm center of the storm. He's never seemed worried, or stressed or afraid. He's always been totally in charge.

But now something is different. When Jesus gets to the garden, he falls on his face, with tears rolling down his cheeks. "Father," he starts to pray desperately. "Please… is there any other way?" The story in Luke says he was "in great agony" and "his sweat became like great drops of blood falling down to the ground." All of a sudden, Jesus doesn't seem so calm and in charge anymore. It almost looks like Jesus is the one freaking out.

Wait... *Jesus* freaking out?? What in the world is happening? How could the One who controls weather and demons and sickness and death be freaking out? What could he be scared of? Do you think he's scared of dying on the cross? Do you think he's scared of how much it's going to hurt? After all, it is going to hurt... a lot.

I don't think that's what Jesus is freaking out about. After all, Jesus is the bravest, strongest person who has ever lived. And there have been plenty of people who have bravely faced death before. I don't think Jesus is suddenly chickening out here.

Here's what's going on: Jesus knows that the worst thing that is going to happen tomorrow isn't the nails or the spear or the crown of thorns. Those are all bad, but they aren't the worst thing. The worst thing is that on the cross, Jesus is going to be punished by his Father for all the bad things you and I have ever done. The Bible says that the punishment for disobeying God is hell: pain and torment and God's anger and separation from God forever. (That's because disobeying God is a really, *really* big deal; it's the worst thing you can possibly do, and so it deserves the worst possible punishment). And that's the punishment that Jesus is going to endure on the cross. I deserve to go to hell forever because of all the bad things that I've done. The same goes for you too. And on the cross, Jesus is going to endure all of my hell and all of your hell and all of the hell for every single person who will ever trust in him. Think of it: millions and millions of everlasting hells descending on Jesus all at once, the punishment for all the sins of all God's children all put onto Jesus. When he prays, "Father, let this cup pass from me," that's the "cup" he's talking about: the cup of God's punishment of sin, the cup of hell.

That's why he's in agony and scared and crying. Hell is the most terrifying thing in the world. How do I know? Because even *Jesus* is afraid of it.

But right here, at this moment, we don't just see how scary hell is; we also see just how much God loves us. Because this was the plan all along: you and I deserve hell, and so Jesus endures hell for us, in our place, so that we can go free and enjoy God's blessing and love and presence forever. 1 John 4:10 says it this way: "This is love: not that we have loved God (because we haven't), but that he loved us and sent his Son to be the wrath-absorbing sacrifice for our sins."

That's why he prays, "Father, if this cannot pass unless I drink it, your will be done." What he means is, "If this cannot pass *from them*—if there's no other way to forgive their sin and take away their hell—then I'll do it."

Can you imagine being loved that much? This scene here in the garden is proof of how much he loves you, how far he is willing to go for you. Jesus takes all your punishment, all your sin, all your hell... because he loves you.

The King on the cross

Two other men, both criminals, were also led out with him to be executed. When they came to the place called the Skull, they crucified him there, along with the criminals—one on his right, the other on his left. Jesus said, "Father, forgive them, for they do not know what they are doing." And they divided up his clothes by casting lots.
The people stood watching, and the rulers even sneered at him. They said, "He saved others; let him save himself if he is God's Messiah, the Chosen One."
The soldiers also came up and mocked him. They offered him wine vinegar and said, "If you are the king of the Jews, save yourself." There was a written notice above him, which read: this is the king of the Jews. –Luke 23:32-38

Has anyone ever asked you what you want to be when you grow up? Maybe you want to be a teacher, or a airline pilot, or a doctor or an astronaut. Maybe, if you're really ambitious, you want to be a princess or a unicorn.

Well, a lot of people end up doing something when they grow up that's entirely different than what they had planned when they were a kid. But some people end up doing exactly what they always wanted to do. And the reason that those kids who wanted to be astronauts or teachers grow up to be astronauts or teachers isn't just because they were lucky; no, it's because they planned and worked hard to make it happen. The little boy who grew up to be an astronaut didn't just sit around waiting for NASA to call him; he went to space camp and later went to college and joined the air force or whatever it is you do to become an astronaut. He had a plan and he made it happen.

Jesus had a plan, too. Even before he was born, even before the world had been made, he had this plan: he knew exactly what he wanted to do when he grew up. But his plan wasn't something fun like being an astronaut. His plan was to die on the cross.

"Why would he plan that?" you might think. Wouldn't it make more sense to do the exact opposite: to plan how to *not* die? After all, I don't sit at home dreaming up gruesome ways I hope I die.

But this was Jesus' plan all along. Because his plan was so much bigger than just himself. The cross was planned to do something amazing, something only God could do: to rescue sinners and punish their sin at the same time.

You see, God loves sinners passionately; he loves you and me more than we could ever even dream.

Even though we disobey him and try to live without him and rob his glory and ignore his rule, he still loves us and still wants us in his family. He still invites us to come into his kingdom party.

But at the same time, God is holy, which means that he refuses to tolerate sin, and sinners cannot even come near him. He is a good judge, and good judges are tough on crime. He won't just sweep sin under the rug, wink at our badness, and let things go. If he did that, he wouldn't be a good judge. In fact, he wouldn't be God.

So how can God rescue the sinners that he loves while still being tough on crime and punishing sin? By sending his Son to take the place of sinners, to take their punishment so that they can go free. It would be like if you were guilty of murder and were about to be thrown in jail, but the father of the person you killed stepped forward and said, "I'll go to jail for you." That's how crazy God's love for you is. Jesus stepped forward to take your punishment so that you could go free. And he did it simply because he loves you.

And so this was the plan all along. Everything that we've seen Jesus doing and saying has all been leading to this moment, when the nails go through his hands. This is what everything has been about. Think about it: Jesus touching the untouchable leper because he loves those that no one else does; Jesus forgiving the paralyzed man; Jesus inviting himself over to Zacchaeus's house; Jesus telling stories about God rejoicing over sinners;

Jesus coming not as a king but as a lowly baby to lowly people. All these stories are just pictures of the rescue mission, different ways we see Jesus loving the last people you'd expect him to. Every miracle Jesus did, every story Jesus told, every person Jesus helped, were all just steps along the road to the cross, to show us Jesus' sacrificial love and humility and grace and kindness, so that when we come to the cross we'd see that this is the greatest rescue of them all. Because this is where Jesus was going all along: to rescue you.

The Most Natural Thing in the World

On the first day of the week, very early in the morning, the women took the spices they had prepared and went to the tomb. They found the stone rolled away from the tomb, but when they entered, they did not find the body of the Lord Jesus. While they were wondering about this, suddenly two men in clothes that gleamed like lightning stood beside them. In their fright the women bowed down with their faces to the ground, but the men said to them, "Why do you look for the living among the dead? He is not here; he has risen! Remember how he told you, while he was still with you in Galilee: 'The Son of Man must be delivered over to the hands of sinners, be crucified and on the third day be raised again.' " Then they remembered his words.
When they came back from the tomb, they told all these things to the Eleven and to all the others. It was Mary Magdalene, Joanna, Mary the mother of James, and the others with them who told this to the apostles. But they did not believe the women, because their words seemed to them like nonsense. Peter, however, got up and ran to the tomb. Bending over, he saw the strips of linen lying by themselves, and he went away, wondering to himself what had happened.
–Luke 24:1-12

Have you ever been to a funeral of someone you knew and loved? Or have you ever had a pet die? In those really sad moments, sometimes people will say something which they mean to be helpful, but isn't actually. Sometimes, in an effort to be helpful and kind, people will say, "Death is a normal, natural part of life," and maybe add something about "the circle of life" like something out of The Lion King. What they probably mean is, "Everyone and everything dies, so you shouldn't feel too bad." Why they think that would be helpful, I don't know. At least they're trying.

But not only is that not really helpful, it's also not true. Death is not a normal, natural part of life. Yes, everyone and everything dies. But that doesn't make it normal and natural. Death is proof that something has gone very, very wrong with the world. Back at the beginning, God didn't set up a world in which things die and break and fall apart and are sad. God made us to live forever, to never be sick or lonely or sad. That's what's natural; that's what's normal. Sin has ruined everything and messed up the world God has made. It's been this way for so long that it seems like it's always been this way, but it hasn't. The fact that things die is very *unnatural*.

So when we come to the greatest miracle in the history of the world—the resurrection of Jesus—in one sense it's amazing and surprising and unexpected. I mean, after all, no one else in the history of the world has raised *himself* back to life. That's a pretty neat trick. But in another sense, maybe the resurrection of Jesus shouldn't surprise us. Maybe we could even say that the resurrection of Jesus is finally something *natural* happening, instead of unnatural. The fact that the King of kings and the Author of life beat death and rose from the grave is the most natural thing in the world. *Of course* he beat death: he was the One who invented life. *Of course* he didn't stay dead: the wages of sin is death, and he didn't have any sin he had to pay for. *Of course* he rose from the dead: there was no possible way for Death to keep the King dead.

So on Easter, when we celebrate the resurrection, what we're really celebrating is that something normal happened for once: death didn't win. We're celebrating God starting to turn this backwards, upside-down world right-ways up again.

Because, you see, Jesus' resurrection was just the beginning, not the end. Just like when he brought Lazarus back to life to give us a little picture of the future breaking into the present, Jesus' own resurrection is another look at what the future is going to be like. One day, Death will be finally get kicked out of the universe. One day, God will finish putting things right-ways up. One day, everyone who loves Jesus will be alive and free and full of happiness with him forever and ever. One day, life will be normal again. And Easter is the proof of that.

The Best Prank Ever

Now that same day two of them were going to a village called Emmaus, about seven miles from Jerusalem. They were talking with each other about everything that had happened. As they talked and discussed these things with each other, Jesus himself came up and walked along with them; but they were kept from recognizing him. He asked them, "What are you discussing together as you walk along?"

They stood still, their faces downcast. One of them, named Cleopas, asked him, "Are you the only one visiting Jerusalem who does not know the things that have happened there in these days?"

"What things?" he asked.

"About Jesus of Nazareth," they replied. "He was a prophet, powerful in word and deed before God and all the people. The chief priests and our rulers handed him over to be sentenced to death, and they crucified him; but we had hoped that he was the one who was going to redeem Israel. And what is more, it is the third day since all this took place. In addition, some of our women amazed us. They went to the tomb early this morning but didn't find his body. They came and told us that they had seen a vision of angels, who said he was alive.

Then some of our companions went to the tomb and found it just as the women had said, but they did not see Jesus."
He said to them, "How foolish you are, and how slow to believe all that the prophets have spoken! Did not the Messiah have to suffer these things and then enter his glory?" And beginning with Moses and all the Prophets, he explained to them what was said in all the Scriptures concerning himself.
As they approached the village to which they were going, Jesus continued on as if he were going farther. But they urged him strongly, "Stay with us, for it is nearly evening; the day is almost over." So he went in to stay with them.
When he was at the table with them, he took bread, gave thanks, broke it and began to give it to them. Then their eyes were opened and they recognized him, and he disappeared from their sight. They asked each other, "Were not our hearts burning within us while he talked with us on the road and opened the Scriptures to us?"
–Luke 24:13-32

Have you ever pulled a prank on someone? A prank is a type of joke where you trick your friends into thinking one thing's happening, even though something else funny is happening instead. When they realize what's really going on, everyone laughs.

Did you know that Jesus pulled a prank once? This is the story of Jesus, right after his resurrection, pulling a prank on two of his friends.

The same day that Jesus rose back to life, two of his friends were walking home. They were very sad—after all, they had seen Jesus killed just a few days before. They had thought he was the Savior and the King, but now he was dead and all their dreams were crushed. Plus, they had lost their friend. No wonder they were so sad.

So Jesus decided to surprise them ("Ta da! I'm not dead anymore!"), but to do it in a sneaky, almost funny, way. He could have just showed himself right away (which is what he did with the other disciples), but he decided to have some fun with these two friends. So as they were walking along the road, Jesus came up to them, but they didn't recognize him. Maybe he was in disguise, or maybe he used his power to keep them from recognizing him.

Either way, however he did it, he walked up in disguise and said, "Hi guys, what's up? Why are you so sad?"

They looked at each other, surprised. Who was this guy? Didn't everybody know what had just happened? So they told him all about their friend Jesus, how they had hoped he was the king, but that he was dead now. They hung their heads, sad all over again.

Jesus was probably smiling at this point. His joke was going perfectly. "Come on, dummies!" Jesus said gently (of course, he was smiling as he said this, because he wasn't being mean—this was all part of the joke). "Haven't you read your Bibles? Don't you realize that this is exactly what the Bible said would happen: that the King would suffer and die and then come back to life!"

His two friends were still confused. (If you've ever been on the receiving end of a prank, you were probably confused at first too). So Jesus started a little Bible study with them, right there as they walked down the road. He began explaining how all the stories and prophecies in the Old Testament all pointed forward to him. And as he talked, a deep, quiet joy started to grow in his friends' hearts, warming them up from the inside out. They started to understand; they began, for the first time, to see—*really* see, with the eyes of their heart — what kind of Savior Jesus was. And their hearts, filling up with happiness, soon were overflowing. Their tears were gone; now they were excited. (One thing to notice about Jesus' prank: the point of the joke was to make them feel *better* in the end).

As they approached their home, Jesus' joke continued. He pretended that he was going to keep going on his way, but the two friends (who *still* didn't recognize him) insisted that he stay for dinner (which was what Jesus really planned to do). At dinner, Jesus picked up the bread and broke it and thanked God for it, which is exactly what he always did at every meal. And at that moment—maybe it was the way he broke the bread, or maybe he took off his disguise, or maybe he just let them see him for real—the friends recognized him. "Jesus!" they cried out with happiness. Jesus winked... and vanished.

His friends sat there, stunned for a moment, and then excitedly jumped up. "Did you see that!" "I somehow knew it was him—he's the only person who can make us feel that happy!" "We've got to go tell everyone else!" And even though it was late, they ran all the way back to Jerusalem to spread the word that Jesus was alive.

Best. prank. ever.

Right?

The Half-Empty Glass

Now Thomas (also known as Twin), one of the Twelve, was not with the disciples when Jesus came. So the other disciples told him, "We have seen the Lord!"
But he said to them, "Unless I see the nail marks in his hands and put my finger where the nails were, and put my hand into his side, I will not believe."
A week later his disciples were in the house again, and Thomas was with them. Though the doors were locked, Jesus came and stood among them and said, "Peace be with you!" Then he said to Thomas, "Put your finger here; see my hands. Reach out your hand and put it into my side. Stop doubting and believe."
Thomas said to him, "My Lord and my God!"
Then Jesus told him, "Because you have seen me, you have believed; blessed are those who have not seen and yet have believed." –John 20:24-29

You may have heard the expression, "Glass half full" or "Glass half empty." The expression means that if you fill up a glass halfway, there are two kinds of people: the kind of people who see the glass as half empty (which means they focus on the bad side of things, how the glass is missing water), or half full (which means they focus on the good side of things, how the glass has water in it). *Optimists* are people who tend to focus on the good side of things. *Pessimists* are people who tend to focus on the bad side of things.

Remember Thomas, from when we met Jesus' twelve disciples? Thomas was a pessimist, which meant that he was always quick to see the bad side of things. He usually assumed that things would go wrong, and was the last person to believe good news. He was sort of like Eeyore, from *Winne the Pooh*—"It's probably going to rain today," Eeyore would always say gloomily. Thomas was the Eeyore of the group.

Once, Jesus was on his way to Jerusalem, which was sort of dangerous because all the Pharisees there wanted him dead. All of the disciples were nervous about going to Jerusalem, and it was Thomas who spoke up first. "Well, we might as well go die with him, I suppose." Spoken like a true pessimist.

Later, at Jesus' final dinner with his disciples, he was telling them how he would soon be going to heaven to prepare an everlasting home for them. "I will come back and take you to be with me that you also may be where I am. You know the way to the place where I am going," Jesus said.

Thomas didn't understand what in the world Jesus was talking about, so he whined, "Lord, we don't even know where you're going. So how in the world would we know how to get there?"

Yep, Thomas was a pessimist all right. But Jesus loves pessimists (and optimists and every other kind of sinner, too). So when Jesus rose back to life, he had a special plan for Thomas.

The first time Jesus appeared to his disciples after the resurrection, Thomas wasn't there. So the next time they saw Thomas, they all told him excitedly, "Jesus is alive! We've seen him with our own eyes!"

What do you think Thomas thought? Do you think he quickly believed the good news, and got excited and happy that Jesus was alive?

Nope. Good ol' Eeyore Thomas had a hard time believing good news. "Unless I see the nail marks with my own eyes, and touch him with my own hands, I'll never believe," Thomas said grumpily.

A week later, all the disciples were together again, and this time Thomas was with them. And suddenly, there was Jesus! Everyone else was happy, but Thomas' jaw dropped open.

Jesus smiled gently at Thomas. "You wanted to see and touch? Okay, here I am. Touch the nail marks in my hands. Touch the wound in my side. Stop doubting, and trust me."

Thomas fell to his knees. "My Lord and my God!" he said with wide-eyed wonder.

And when Thomas got up off his knees, he was a different person. No longer was the cup half-empty. And it wasn't hall-full either. For the rest of his life, Thomas would eagerly tell everyone he met that, in the words of Psalm 23, "My cup overflows!" Jesus' resurrection changed everything—it meant everything Jesus said was true, and every one of God's promises was real, and that sin and death were beaten, and that there was hope and joy and strength for the future no matter what happened. Jesus' resurrection changed everything, and that changed Thomas too.

Jesus on the Loose

Then the eleven disciples went to Galilee, to the mountain where Jesus had told them to go. When they saw him, they worshiped him; but some doubted. Then Jesus came to them and said, "All authority in heaven and on earth has been given to me. Therefore go and make disciples of all nations, baptizing them in the name of the Father and of the Son and of the Holy Spirit, and teaching them to obey everything I have commanded you. And surely I am with you always, to the very end of the age." –Matthew 28:16-20

Jesus had finished everything he had come to do: he died to pay for sins, he had beaten death and risen back to life, he had introduced people to God and brought his kingdom to earth. Now it was time for Jesus to return to his Father in heaven. But before he left, he had important directions to give his disciples. Because even though Jesus' earthly mission was finished, his job wasn't actually over. Not by a long shot. In fact, it was just beginning.

"All authority in heaven and on earth has been given to me," Jesus told them. What that means is,

"I'm the King of the whole world now—even if people don't know it yet. I went up against sin and death and Satan, and I won. Nothing can stop me now."

Jesus is the unstoppable King... so now what? That's what Jesus said next: "Therefore, go and make disciples of all nations." "I'm King of the whole world... now go tell the whole world that. Everyone needs to know how I won. My kingdom needs to spread everywhere now."

In all of Jesus' miracles when he was on earth, we were able to see glimpses of the Kingdom coming. Everywhere Jesus went, sin and sickness and sadness started going away, and forgiveness and life and joy started taking their place. But Jesus was just one person (even though he is God); when he was walking around on earth, he could only be in one place at a time. So the Kingdom started off looking really small: it was just the King walking around freeing people. But now that Jesus was going back to heaven, the Kingdom was going to start blowing up. Jesus was going to live in the hearts of every single person who trusted him, so that the Kingdom could start spreading fast. Jesus going back to heaven didn't mean he was going away; it meant that Jesus was now on the loose.

That's what he told his disciples: "I am with you always, to the very end of the age." Even though they wouldn't see Jesus anymore, he would still be with them, and would be living in them. And now Jesus' mission would become their mission:

spreading his Kingdom all over the world. Everywhere they went, sin and sickness and sadness would start to go away, and forgiveness and life and joy would start to take their place. Now Jesus could start working all over the place, through all the people who loved him.

Today, all these years later, Jesus is still on the loose, and his kingdom is still spreading. And everywhere the kingdom spreads, forgiveness and life and joy spreads with it. All over the world, sin and death and Satan are on the retreat (even when it sometimes looks like they're winning), because people who love Jesus are laying down their lives and loving people and telling people the good news about him. Every time a person puts their trust in Jesus, they get added to the kingdom and Jesus comes to make his home in their hearts. And the kingdom party just keeps getting bigger and bigger.

The King Sits Down

After he had provided purification for sins, he sat down at the right hand of the Majesty in heaven. – Hebrews 1:3

After giving his disciples the mission, Jesus rose up into the clouds and disappeared into heaven, leaving them behind. But then what? What did Jesus do next? Sometimes I like to imagine what it must have been like in heaven on the day that Jesus came home to his Father.

Imagine the celebration that must have been going on in heaven. King Jesus had finished everything he had gone to earth to do, and now was coming home. All the angels were probably lined up to greet him, dressed in their best angel clothes (do angels change their clothes?). As Jesus entered heaven's gates, trumpets sounded, and all the hosts of heaven raised a shout of triumph that shook the whole place. "Three cheers for the conquering King! Long live the King!" And as Jesus walked up heaven's golden street, he no longer looked like an ordinary man; his face shone like a thousand suns, and the angel armies knelt in worship and shielded their eyes from the brightness of his glory.

But as he passed by, the angels whispered to one another in awe: his hands were still scarred from the nails of the cross. Although Jesus had taken back all the divine power and glory that he had laid aside when he first became a man, the marks of his pain and death were still there. Forever and ever, those scars would remain as a reminder of what he had suffered, and the victory he had won.

A new song of praise swept through the angelic host: "Worthy is the Lamb who was slain to receive power and wealth and wisdom and strength and honor and glory and praise!"

Jesus approached the throne of heaven and looked up to see his Father, smiling the biggest smile the universe has ever known. "Well done, my beloved Son," came the voice of thunder from the throne. "Welcome home."

Jesus stepped up to the throne. There was his crown, glittering with a beauty far beyond what any earthly king could imagine, which Jesus had first laid aside when he became a man. Jesus knelt before his Father, as his Father raised the crown and placed it on Jesus' head: the same head which, only a few weeks before, had worn a mocking crown of thorns. This, at last, was the crown that Jesus deserved. And all of heaven erupted in song and praise and glad shouting yet again, even louder than the first time.

And then, the newly-crowned King of the universe did what any king who has won a battle and conquered his enemies does: he sat down on his throne. His work was accomplished; sin had been paid for, and Satan had been defeated and was on the run. Now Jesus' kingdom would be unstoppable, because once again the King was on his throne.

WIJD?

He must reign until he has put all his enemies under his feet. The last enemy to be destroyed is death. -1 Corinthians 15:25-26

Have you ever heard the phrase WWJD? Back when I was a kid, they used to print "WWJD" on tie-dyed bracelets that all the youth group kids would wear. (Do they still do that? I don't know; I'm must be getting old). "WWJD" stands for a question: What Would Jesus Do? The idea was, when you were facing a difficult situation—maybe someone had said something unkind to you, or maybe you needed to tell the truth, or maybe doing the right thing was going to be hard—you would ask yourself, "What would Jesus do?" And you would think about how he would respond if he was in your shoes, and then you would do what you think he would do.

WWJD is a great question; we're supposed to love people just like Jesus loved them, so if you follow Jesus, you should always be asking yourself what Jesus would do if we were in your shoes.

There's a problem with the question, though.

"What Would Jesus Do" kind of makes it sound like Jesus isn't around anymore and isn't doing stuff anymore, so we have to think of what he would have done if he were alive today. And of course, that's not quite right: Jesus is in fact alive today, and is doing lots of things.

So I've got an idea for a new question. Instead of just asking WWJD—what would Jesus do; let's ask WIJD—what is Jesus doing? Because if Jesus really did rise from the dead, that means he's alive and active and doing stuff today. And if we know what he's doing, then we can get on board with it and join him.

So what is Jesus doing today? There are a lot of ways that the Bible answers that question (because there are a lot of things that Jesus is doing). Let's just focus on one thing: Jesus is reigning in heaven and making sure his Kingdom keeps advancing.

Right now, at this moment, every molecule and planet and galaxy holds together because Jesus tells it to (see Hebrews 1:2). That's how powerful King Jesus is. Sitting on the throne, he is making sure that planet Earth keeps spinning, and the sun keeps shining, and gravity keeps working. If Jesus stopped being king, everything in the whole universe would immediately spin out of control. So we can be very glad that Jesus is reigning on his throne.

But King Jesus isn't just up in heaven making sure

the molecules all behave. He is also making sure that nothing can stop the mission he gave his first disciples—to spread his Kingdom across the whole world. Right now while you're reading this, he is working on the other side of the world, in countries like China and India and Saudi Arabia, so that people hear about him and put their trust in him. Jesus' kingdom is spreading in those places, and even though many people don't want anything to do with Jesus' kingdom, they can't stop him. His kingdom is coming, whether they like it or not. After all, he's the King! And sin and death and sadness, which sometimes seem like they're in control, are being rolled back as more and more people discover the forgiveness and life and joy in Jesus' kingdom.

But Jesus isn't just working over on the other side of the world. He's working right here too. In your church, his Word is being preached, and people are learning to say sorry for their sins and to trust and love Jesus more. People are telling their friends and families about how great Jesus is. And though many don't want to believe in Jesus, some do, and Jesus' kingdom keeps advancing. People are finding forgiveness and freedom and new life. Sin and death and sadness are being rolled back here, too.

Even when bad things happen—and in this broken world, bad things still happen a lot—King Jesus is still in charge. In fact, the King made an absolutely incredible promise to everyone who trusts and loves him: he has promised to make every bad thing turn out for good in the end. Sometimes it's hard to believe that, and sometimes it's hard to see how all the bad things turn out good in the end, but King Jesus promised it, so we can believe it.

One day, when his kingdom has reached every nation and language and people group, King Jesus will return and will kick sin and death and sadness out forever. But until then, nothing and no one will be able stop his kingdom. In the end, Jesus wins, and everyone who is on his team wins as well. He promised that, too.

The King coming Back

The Lord himself will come down from heaven, with a loud command, with the voice of the archangel and with the trumpet call of God, and the dead in Christ will rise first. After that, we who are still alive and are left will be caught up together with them in the clouds to meet the Lord in the air. And so we will be with the Lord forever. Therefore, encourage one another with these words. -1 Thessalonians 4:16-18

What's your favorite book or movie? I think one of the things that makes the difference between "just okay" stories and "awesome" stories is how they end. There's nothing worse than coming to the end of a book or movie and then finding out that the ending is lame. But if the ending is surprising, or exciting, or wonderful, it makes the whole story worth it.

One of my favorite book/movie trilogies is *The Lord of the Rings*. I like the first two books, but my favorite is the third one, because the ending is epic. Like seriously, over the top, cheering-on-the-good-guys epic. It makes the whole 9-hour movie marathon worth it to see the bad guys defeated and the good guys win in such an awesome way.

The story of Jesus has an awesome ending. It has an awesome beginning and middle too, of course, but the ending is really what makes the whole story worth it.

Think back to how the story has gone so far: the true King arrives in an upside-down, backwards way—not as a conquering hero but as a helpless baby. He has come to put everything right-ways up again. And as he begins his ministry, we start to see what his Kingdom looks like: a celebration party of forgiveness and life and joy that starts small and keeps spreading. He loves the unlovable, and touches the untouchable, and forgives the unforgivable. He proves that he has power over everything that he has made; even wind and waves obey his word. Everywhere he goes, the future starts breaking in early: the dead come back to life, the sick are healed, the sinners are forgiven.

And then comes the twist: this King has come to conquer sin and death, but in the most surprising way. He will conquer by being conquered; he will kill death by being killed himself. He takes our sin and suffers the punishment that we deserve, all so that we can be forgiven.

And then the tables turn, and death starts working in reverse: the grave spits out the Author of Life, and the King kicks down the gates of hell from the inside out, and comes back to life, having conquered sin and death and Satan once and for all. He ascends back to heaven, sits down on his throne, and begins the march of his kingdom across the world.

One day, that march will be done. People from every nation and tribe and language will have heard about King Jesus and put their trust in him. And when that day comes, the end of the story will come: the King himself will return. The skies will rip open, and we will see King Jesus coming back, shining with glory brighter than the sun. Every person who has ever lived will be raised back to life and will assemble before the King. Every knee will bow—some gladly, some grudgingly—and everyone will proclaim that Jesus Christ really is the Lord of all. Everyone who has rebelled and rejected him will be cast away from him forever, and everyone who trusts and loves him will be gathered into his finally-arriving kingdom. The whole world, which has been broken by sin and stained with tears, will be remade to be a perfect home for God's children again.

And that's when the kingdom party—the kingdom party that started with Jesus turning water into wine—will begin for real. Because now, everything sad will be gone forever: no more sickness or crying or death or pain or sin ever again. Everything will be new and beautiful again, even more than it was at the beginning. And all God's children—everyone who has put their trust in Jesus—will celebrate and sing and dance and thank God for how much he has loved them.

And we will live there with the King, working alongside him, celebrating his goodness, enjoying his love, forever and ever. And it will turn out that this isn't the end of the story, after all; it's only the beginning, because Jesus' love and Jesus' glory and Jesus' kingdom will never end. Every day the party will be more wonderful, every day there will be new adventures and new experiences and new relationships and new happiness, and each day will be better than the one before it, forever and ever and without any end in sight. And forever we will be so glad that Jesus came to rescue us.

What a story! What a kingdom! What a King! Come, Lord Jesus—come back soon!